RED, WHITE, AND BLUEBLOODS

In Frontier Florida

By Malcolm B. Johnson
Editor, The Tallahassee Democrat

Published by the Rotary Clubs of Tallahassee
P. O. Box 3221
Tallahassee, Florida 32302

To
Dorothy Burt Johnson
My Wife
For contributing not only
inspiration, but information—
plus authorship of the Murat and
Wirt chapters, and the title.

Preface

The author is not a historian, only a spinner of historical yarns. Some in this book are twice-told tales, some all but untold.

The professional historian on the project has been Clara Lee Wolfe. She has challenged questionable statements, authenticated them or discarded them. Hers is the contribution to historical research by careful verification, annotation and indexing.

Our purpose has been to produce a book which gives the casual reader a glimpse of some of the characters who converted Florida from a Spanish colony into an American state. At the same time, we hope the footnotes at the back of each chapter may help you, as well as the student of history, find more knowledge in the source books (many long out of print) from which we have drawn our information.

Table of Contents

Introduction

American independence arrived half a century late to Florida.

But the blood of founding patriots ran strong in the veins of pioneers who moved into the new territory when it opened up—just as our nation approached its 50th anniversary:

Thomas Jefferson's grandson was Tallahassee's first reform mayor.

Alexander Hamilton, Jr., ran for delegate to Congress in territorial Florida's first full-term election but lost.

A grandson of Patrick Henry is buried at Quincy.

George Washington's great-grandniece came and married Napoleon Bonaparte's nephew in the Florida capital's eighth wedding.

The name of "Tallahassee" is said to have been chosen for the new Florida capital by the granddaughter of a signer of the Declaration of Independence. Her father, George Walton, Jr., was the first Florida Secretary of State.

Title abstracts to most property in the whole northeast quadrant of modern Tallahassee go back to ownership by the Marquis de Lafayette, who late in life was given a block six miles square for his services as a young man in the American revolution.

In the turbulent politics of the new Florida territory—and in the valiant effort to establish a society in keeping with ancestral position—the personal influences of Jefferson, Madison, Monroe, Andrew Jackson, perhaps even of Aaron Burr, were strong. Naturally, sometimes such influences seemed to conflict, but, all in all, old animosities appeared to dissolve in a common new struggle for survival and success. None of these men of

Revolutionary times ever saw Florida—except Jackson, who was captured by the British as a 13-year-old revolutionary militiaman. He raided Spanish Pensacola in 1814, led a controversial foray into the Tallahassee area in 1818 and three years later took over the territory legally as its first American governor.

But their progeny, their kin, their disciples, neighbors and chroniclers came and played roles in planting United States government in what for most of three centuries had been an alien wilderness.

This is their story.

Who were they? Why did they come? What did they do? How well did they uphold their heroic heritage?

But, first, a bit of background from standard history—

Chapter One

The First Rush

Florida, held by Spain from 1513 to 1763, sat out the American revolution as two puny provinces of the British crown with governors at the hamlet capitals of St. Augustine and Pensacola.

The Apalachicola river separated East Florida from West Florida; and the whole of it, while remaining loyal to Britain during the revolt of older English colonies to the north, played little part in the conflict.[1]

Britain acquired the Floridas from Spain in 1763 in trade for Havana, Cuba, which the English had captured.

The Floridas remained British territory for only 20 years. After losing her other eastern seaboard colonies in the war for American independence, Britain traded Florida back to Spain for the Bahamas by the Treaty of Paris, which also gave Gibraltar to England.

Florida, especially the Apalachee country which Tallahassee centers, probably had fewer human inhabitants in 1776 than at any other time in the past 500 years.

The Spanish explorers De Narvaez and De Soto had come through Apalachee before the middle of the 16th century. De Narvaez launched a disastrous sea trip to Mexico from around Apalachee Bay in 1528. De Soto spent the winter of 1539-40 near present Tallahassee enroute to his discovery of the Mississippi river, and his death. Their exploits have been well-known in Spanish and English history for four centuries.

After De Soto passed through, it was about a century before the Spanish began to pay much attention to Apalachee.

The Spanish had come to plunder, not to plow. Florida, it turned out, had no gold or silver to plunder. So the little colony at St. Augustine was no more than a foothold to preserve nominal control of the Spanish Main. Assignment to the garrison and governance of the Spanish colony of Florida was almost like banishment to an existence of writing plaintive letters for food and money, then long and frustrating waits for unsatisfactory answers and occasional ships carrying replacements or provisions.

In 1639, Spanish Franciscan monks began a string of missions through Apalachee—surrounding modern Tallahassee and serving the fort and port at St. Marks. Their purpose was to tap the agricultural resources of the Apalachee Indians, as well as to Christianize them. Apalachee thus became a breadbasket for the Spanish garrison at St. Augustine, which remained a military outpost while English settlers to the north were busy establishing plantations and prosperous, permanent colonies of English-speaking people.

Apalachee thrived for more than 60 years in a peaceful alliance of industrious Christianized Indians and Spanish missionaries.

That era came to an abrupt end in 1704 when Col. James Moore of South Carolina raised a renegade force of a few Englishmen and a thousand warlike Cherokees for a sweep through Apalachee.

They burned mission after mission, slaughtered hundreds of peaceful Apalachees, and took nearly all the others away into slavery. The remnants of the Apalachees moved westward to Louisiana and disappeared.[2] Moore, who had lost the governorship of South Carolina over a futile attack on St. Augustine in 1702, failed to regain favor by his unauthorized foray against Apalachee. He disappeared into the pages of history.

But the desolation he wrought made Apalachee lapse again into more than a century of wilderness worse than earlier Spanish explorers had found.

The Spanish didn't entirely abandon Apalachee. After 1708, no Spanish missions outside St. Augustine remained. But, as Charlton Tebeau reveals in his *History of Florida*, the Spanish Junta Guerra de Indias in 1716 advocated moving the capital from St. Augustine to Apalachee.[3] Two years later, the fort at St. Marks was rebuilt. However, relocation of the capital became only prophetic.

Gen. Andrew Jackson
Military Governor, 1821
his rule was "simple
and energetic"

William P. Duval
first civil governor
1822-1834
man on the move

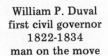

Territorial Capitol
Francis de Castelnau sketch, 1842

By the time the British took possession of Florida in 1763, the farms of Indians destroyed by Moore's raids had long been abandoned. Their outlines remained, though. Gradually the few traders and travelers who passed through Apalachee between St. Augustine, Pensacola, and St. Marks adopted as landmarks the Indian "old fields" or "abandoned villages" (which is what the word "Tallahassee" meant in Indian language).

When Spain ceded Florida to the United States in 1819, there were only a few hundred Indians in the Tallahassee area.[4] They were Seminoles—Creeks and Cherokees who had fled to Florida under American pressure to the north, mixed with a few runaway slaves. To them, the farm lands of Apalachee were "Tallahassee." Even one of the village chiefs went by that name.

The first Territorial Council met at Pensacola in 1822 to set up an American government for Florida. The East Florida delegation came by ship around the tip of Florida, one delegate was drowned in a storm in the northern Gulf of Mexico, and the others were blown ashore near Mobile; they arrived at Pensacola weeks late. Five of the 13 delegates didn't make it to the opening session.[5]

One of the Council's first acts was to send a memorial to President James Monroe asking for the U.S. Corps of Engineers to mark out a road between the two old capitals and "to solicit some suitable place, in the Mickasuky Country or on the Suwanny River or the adjacent country for the permanent seat of Government of Florida".[6]

Council members told the president such a road would pass "through a healthy fine country," which they were "induced to believe for fertility is not surpassed by any land in the southern country."[7]

When nothing came of the plea to Washington, the Council, at its 1823 session in St. Augustine, directed Dr. William H. Simmons of East Florida and John Lee Williams of West Florida to explore the territory between the Suwannee and the Apalachicola rivers for a capital site.

They met near the old fields of Tallahassee as directed, toured around, and finally came back to choose a spot near a pristine ravine, with cascading waters, as the proper place for the seat of government.

On March 4, 1824, Gov. William P. Duval formally proclaimed as the site of the new capital a spot "about a mile southwest from the old deserted fields of Tallahassee, about a half mile south of the Oke-lock-o-ny and Tallahassee trail, at a point where the old Spanish road is intersected by a small trail running southwardly."[8]

The same proclamation directed the Territorial Council to meet there for its next session, in November, 1824.

Settlers, adventurers, and speculators, along with politicians, began to descend on the fertile wilderness of old Tallahassee. As it has been ever since, politicians led the rush. The planters, tradesmen, adventurers and speculators followed shortly.

After Spain agreed in 1819 to cede Florida to the United States if our nation would take over and settle numerous land claim disputes from the Spanish-English-Spanish turnovers of the previous century, it was almost exactly two years before the actual transfer was made.

So the line for political jobs in the new territory was well formed by July of 1821, when the Spanish flag was pulled down and the Stars and Stripes were hoisted over St. Augustine and Pensacola, the twin capitals, and old St. Marks.

It was wild frontier, offering almost no decent living accommodations for civil officers anywhere in the territory; but the prospects were attractive.

Modern Floridians may like to think the climate here was a lure to men bearing the big names of American patriotism to roles in the development of this new American territory. The fact is, though, that most of them needed jobs.

The War of 1812, ending in 1814, was followed by a severe depression that hit bottom in 1819. What fortunes had been retained or attained since Independence finally was won at Yorktown in 1781 had been severely depleted or wiped out in the panic of 1819.

At the same time, families in the original agricultural states had begun to outgrow ancestral land holdings. Great acreages were divided and redivided among heirs while soil fertility was being depleted from nearly 200 years of drain to grow tobacco and cotton. Some families found their slave holdings and manor expenses exceeding the ability of their fields to support them. They sought more fertile lands, or other occupations.

Moreover, the standing army was cut almost in half after the War of 1812. In 1821, high officers had to choose between severe reduction in rank or resignation to seek civilian employment.[9] Florida offered them an opportunity. James Gadsden, Richard Keith Call, Robert H. Butler, and numerous others dropped out of the army to get and hold jobs in Florida civil government.

Gen. Andrew Jackson, himself, the military governor who formally took over the territory from Spain, was not far removed from that situation. He was the junior of two major generals. The reduced U.S. Army had room for only one. The command went to Gen. Jacob L. Brown.

Jackson was about to leave the army and enter politics.

So it was both expedient and convenient in Washington to assign him the task of taking over Florida from Spain and governing the territory until a proper civilian government could be established. Since it was not known whether Americans would be welcome to the resident Spanish and Indians, it also was considered wise to put a rambunctious ramrod like Old Hickory in charge at the beginning. He was well-known in the territory; for in 1818 he had led a highly questionable expedition into Spanish Florida against marauding Indians. He razed their villages in the Tallahassee area and executed two British traders—Robert Ambrister and Alexander Arbuthnot—at St. Marks after a court martial which caused an international incident and embarrassed Jackson (or should have) even into his administration as president.

Jackson didn't take well to the governorship of Florida. He was impatient to get back to Tennessee and politics. Besides, he didn't relish having the men to hold office under him appointed by President Monroe without much, if any, consultation.

An example of both Monroe's peremptory tone and the eagerness of people with the blood of patriots in their veins to take even minor jobs is revealed by a letter the President wrote to Jackson at Pensacola on May 23, 1821:

> ... I have established two judicial districts, one Judge in each, Pensacola to be the residence of one, & St. Augustine of the other. I have appointed Mr. Fromentin, judge at the former, & Mr. Duvall, at the latter. Both those gentlemen I presume you are acquainted with, the one having served in the Senate from Louisiana, & the other in the house of Rep. from Kentucky....
>
> Mr. Walton of Georgia is secretary at Pensacola, the descendant & Representative of the member of Congress of that name, who voted for & signed the Declaration of Independence; Mr. Worthington of Maryland is Secretary at St. Augustine, a person who acted as political agent of the U. States, some years, at Buenos Ayres & Chile.
>
> Mr. Alex Scott of Maryland is appointed Collector of the Customs, Mr. Steuben Smith of N[ew] York Naval officer, Mr.

Hackley, of Virg[inia] Surveyor, & Mr. Baker of this place Inspector at Pensacola. The first mentioned is a man of considerable literary acquirements, & strict integrity, well connected in this State. The second is the son of Col. Wm. Smith, who was aid de camp to Gen. Washington, in the revolutionary war, & afterwards Secr'y of legation at London, where he married the daughter of Mr. Adams former President. He is the nephew of the present Secr'y of State, & his wife is the sister of Mrs. Adams. Of Mr. Hackley you may have heard, in Spain. His wife is the sister of Govr Randolph of Virg[inia] & Mr. Madison & others our friend, have strongly recommended him to me.

As these persons are I believe literally poor, as is indeed, Mr. Baker, who was formerly consul in Spain & Italy, & in whose favor Mr. Jefferson takes an interest, I wish you to place them, if possible, in some of the public buildings, of which I presume there are some not necessary for your own accommodation. It is, I believe, customary, for the revenue officers to be thus provided, wherever it is practicable, and in no instances, can such provision be more important or indispensible to the parties than at the present.[10]

In the same letter, President Monroe informed Jackson that Col. Robert Butler "lately of your staff is app'td. Col. of the 4th reg. etc. & Major Call retains his rank of Captain in the line. It would have given me pleasure to have placed the latter near you, but on great consideration, I thought better for you as well as for myself, to pursue the course I have done."[11]

Jackson wanted his old aide, Call, for secretary of the territory, but that position went to George Walton, Jr., son of one of Georgia's three signers of the Declaration of Independence. Monroe explained the political practicalities of his choice to Jackson: "Mr. Walton was strongly supported by two senators from Georgia, Mr. Walker and Mr. Elliott, both estimable men—I could do nothing else for him, and Major Call was already provided for."[12]

He closed with a generous presidential back-patting for General Jackson:

I have full confidence, that your appointment will be immediately & most beneficially felt. Smugglers & slave traders will hide their heads; pirates will disappear, & the Seminoles, cease to give us trouble. So effectual will the impression be, that I think, the recollection of your past worries, will smoothe your way as to the future. Past experience shews, that neither of us are without enemies. If you still have any, as may be presumed, they will watch your movements, hoping to find some inadvertent circumstance, to turn against you. Be therefore on your guard. Your country indulges no such feelings. From it you will find, a liberal confidence, & a generous support.

With my best wishes for your welfare, & the best regards of my family for Mrs. Jackson, I am, dear sir,

> your friend & servant,
> James Monroe[13]

Jackson accepted the commission, took over the territory, and exercised virtually dictatorial command (as some situations, indeed, required in the absence of any formal law during a transition from Spanish to American jurisprudence). He told Secretary of State John Quincy Adams he felt his administration "ought to be simple and energetic." It was. He even reduced activities of federal district judges to little more than the authority of justices of the peace, and was backed up from Washington.[14]

As for the appointees sent to him by commission from the nation's capital, Jackson complained to Dr. James C. Bronough, an army surgeon who had served under him and had come down to head Florida's first territorial legislature:

> Had I anticipated this I should have adhered to my first determination not to have accepted the Government, but I will close my official duties with the next Congress as I am determined never to be associated with such men as some of those who are appointed.[15]

Jackson served as military governor of the territory only eight months, from March 12 to Nov. 13, 1821. "I am truly wearied of public life," he said in his letter of resignation. "I want rest, and my private concerns imperiously demand my attention."[16]

He had already been back home in Tennessee for five months, leaving administration of the territory primarily to Secretary George Walton until William P. Duval of Kentucky was moved over from District Judge at St. Augustine to become the first civil governor of the territory on April 17, 1822.

On the score of living conditions alone, Jackson's impatience to be off to Tennessee was understandable. Not in all the Florida he took over from Spain was there a home anywhere near as comfortable as his "Hermitage" in Nashville.

Neither St. Augustine nor Pensacola, where Jackson was stationed, offered much for the highest officers nor members of the nation's most notable families: A letter by Alexander

Hamilton, Jr., from St. Augustine, where he was serving as a land claims commissioner, requested Secretary of State John Quincy Adams for permission to occupy one front room at the government house "during the sickly season."

Nevertheless, men of the higher echelons of American politics vied for Florida positions. A footnote in the published official territorial papers indicates their interest:

> During 1819 and 1820, when expectation was high that the cession in question would be consummated at an early date, many persons were recommended for office—names being proposed for the offices of Governor, Secretary, Judges, Collectors, et cetera. Some of the names proposed were those of men of local prominence, such as the Governors of Maine and North Carolina, Nathaniel Ware, a former Secretary of the territories of Mississippi and Alabama, and William S. Fulton, who was to become in later years successively Secretary and Governor of Arkansas Territory.[17]

And when the government finally was being formed, in 1822, among those who were pushed for the governorship that went to Duval were James P. Preston, former governor of Virginia; John Branch, former governor of North Carolina (who was proposed earlier for Jackson's role in Florida and who later became governor of Florida); William King, who had been a colonel under Jackson in his 1818 expedition into Florida; James Strong, a former congressman from New York; and Joseph L. Smith, another former army colonel.[18]

In this situation, it was only natural that sons, grandsons, relatives and friends of American revolutionary heroes should get appointments and be attracted to private opportunities in the new Florida Territory.

Thomas Jefferson and John Adams were still alive (both died July 4, 1826). President Monroe was a protege of Jefferson and successor to President James Madison, one of Jefferson's closest friends. John Quincy Adams, son of the signer, was Secretary of State and destined to follow Monroe to the presidency. Their attachments and concerns for distressed kin of the patriots of '76 could be taken for granted.

Thus we find that when Tallahassee was chosen as the seat of government in 1824, there was an immigration of descendants of men and women most prominent in the Revolution only 50 years before.

Jefferson's kin were notably involved in settlement and development of the Tallahassee country.

NOTES

1. For an excellent study of the period see J. Leitch Wright, Jr., *Florida in the American Revolution* (Gainesville: University Presses of Florida, 1975).

2. Clarence Edwin Carter, ed., *The Territorial Papers of the United States*, 27 vols. (Washington, D.C.: United States Government Printing Office, 1956), 23:123 (hereafter cited as Carter, *Territorial Papers*).

3. Charlton W. Tebeau, *A History of Florida* (Coral Gables: University of Miami Press, 1971), p. 65 (hereafter cited as Tebeau, *Florida*).

4. Bertram H. Groene, *Ante-Bellum Tallahassee* (Tallahassee: Florida Heritage Foundation, 1971), p. 14 (hereafter cited as Groene, *Tallahassee*).

5. Tebeau, *Florida*, p. 122.

6. Carter, *Territorial Papers*, 22:522-523.

7. Ibid., p. 522.

8. Ibid., pp. 854-855.

9. Ibid., p. 429.

10. Ibid., pp. 55-56.

11. Ibid., p. 56.

12. Ibid.

13. Ibid., p. 57.

14. The former Spanish Governor, Callava, refused to surrender certain papers that Jackson believed to be the property of the new American government. Ignoring Callava's claims of diplomatic immunity, Old Hickory ordered the Spaniard's arrest and seized the papers. Judge Eligius Fromentin issued a writ of habeas corpus for Callava, which Jackson rejected. While the old soldier's conduct toward the new federal judges was a bit high-handed, it was well within Jackson's authority as supreme judge. In contrast, Fromentin's jurisdiction covered only revenue laws and the importation of slaves. For a more complete account of the episode see Herbert J. Doherty, Jr., "The Governorship of Andrew Jackson," *The Florida Historical Quarterly*, 33:3-31.

15. Carter, *Territorial Papers*, 22:52.

16. Ibid., p. 276.

17. Ibid., p. 3.

18. Ibid., p. 469.

Chapter Two

Jefferson's Kin

Francis Eppes was a Jefferson by discipline and descent; but his considerable influence on the capital of territorial Florida was more moral and cultural than political.

Thomas Jefferson, author of the Declaration of Independence, was his grandfather on his mother's side and his great uncle from his father's side of the family. Jefferson exercised a guiding hand on young Francis' education, as he had on the upbringing of his father, John Wayles Eppes, who became a member of Congress from Virginia.[1]

Francis was born at "Eppington" in Chesterfield County, Virginia, in 1801.[2] His mother was Mary (Maria), youngest daughter of Thomas Jefferson. His father, Jack, was a nephew of Jefferson's wife. Jefferson took a fatherly interest in their training and careers as long as he lived. The elder Eppes spent some of his adolescent years in the Jefferson home, and Jefferson's youngest daughter, Maria lived with Eppes' family while Jefferson was minister to France.[3]

Young Francis was 23 when his father died, and only two years older when Jefferson passed away at Monticello on July 4, 1826. He inherited little from his father, who had taken a second wife. Jefferson died bankrupt, but before his death he gave Francis the fine octagonal plantation house, Poplar Forest, which the third president had designed for Eppes' mother but built long after her death as a retreat from the constant visitors who crowded into Monticello for interviews with one of the few remaining patriots of 1776.

However, only a fragment of the worn-out acreage of Poplar Forest came to Eppes. It wasn't enough to support Francis and

Francis Ware Eppes
Grandson of Thomas Jefferson
three times mayor of Tallahassee

Poplar Forest
Eppes left this home in Virginia to resettle in a Florida log house.

Jefferson-Randolph-Eppes Connections

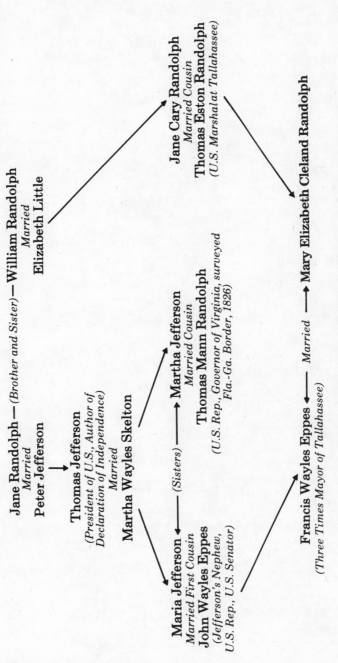

his young family—nor perhaps even to keep his slaves busy. He had bought 20 of them from his grandfather a few years before for $4,000, which gave Jefferson a bit of badly needed cash and enabled him to keep some faithful servants in the family.[4]

Talk of leaving for Florida was contagious among Virginians. On April 1, 1827, Eppes' young wife wrote to the wife of his cousin, Thomas Jefferson Randolph:

.. 'emigration' has been the sole topic of conversation, the one engrossing subject of our sleeping and waking thought. . .

These gullied worn out fields, and this unfinished leaking hull of a house, have become more than ever distasteful to both Francis and myself, and we needed little before to render them altogether odious. Tobacco is the only thing which can be made here, and after vast labour and expense, in raising and manufacturing the vile weed, and acquiring both skill and judgement in the business, to find still that no profit must be expected, is disheartening indeed, and Francis who began with sanguine hopes on the subject, is now as much wearied and sickened with a planters life, as I who from the first abhorred it.

Mama is quite willing to remove, I believe, and the girls wish it exceedingly, and even Papa, who opposed it at first (who would have expected opposition from him, in such a scheme?) Seems now to be coming round, and if what he hears in Albermarle is favorable I doubt not but that he will return to us with his mind made up on the subject.

Florida, Tallahassee and its neighborhood will be our location if matters can be brought to bear, the girls to keep a school, for which we have been informed there is very good opening, which the hire of Papa's few remaining hands will furnish a support for Mama and himself until he can collect sufficient funds to make a small purchase of land; and Francis and myself will settle in a log house in the woods, he to begin life anew as a sugar planter and I as—what? for I know not what my particular avocations will be there, or how I shall employ myself beyond the customary occupation of our unlucky sin in 'making children' as the old Dutch woman expressed it.

I am weary of this state, and of the state of things here, and I feel as if we should all be a regenerated people if we could once, and in body turn our backs on it, and shake off the dust of it from the soles of our feet, but among all my reasons for wishing to go, the greatest is that I think it possible even probable that a warm climate would in some measure restore Mama's health. . .[5]

Within a year after Jefferson's death, Francis loaded up his slaves and made the overland trek to the new frontier of Florida, which was just beginning to attract settlers from old Virginia and the Carolinas. He bought land on Black Creek

about a dozen miles northeast of the capital village, named it
L'Eau Noir plantation, erected a log house and outbuildings,
and settled into the life of a planter.[6]

It was rough living for the young gentry from Virginia; but
though accommodations perhaps were finer where they had
come from, times were rougher.

Eppes' sister-in-law Harriet Randolph, who apparently accompanied his pregnant wife Elizabeth south to Tallahassee a
year after Eppes came down, wrote home to her mother, Mrs.
Thomas Eston Randolph:

> This is a very comfortable house of Francis's, roomy and airy and
> quite good looking for a log pen. The floor of our loft (Mary's and
> mine) is not nailed down, and the seams gape rather more widely
> than is pleasant, but we have remedied the evil by spreading down
> your parlor carpet.
>
> The house is on a little eminence, skirting the barren, but with
> hammock enough around it for beauty and shade. The yard is fenced
> in, and nicely cleared up with only a few trees left standing; at the
> back of it is a fine crop of cotton growing and around the other
> three sides the most splendid growth of forest trees I ever
> beheld—superb oaks covered with the long moss of this country
> which I cannot describe to you. I never even imagined anything so
> beautiful so graceful.[7]

The Randolphs, parents of Elizabeth Cleland Eppes, were
about to join the trek to the Tallahassee country—and Harriet
exulted in the prospect of having the whole family together
again, even while fretting with doubt that her mother could
stand the arduous trip. "Bonapart's Russian campaign could not
have been harder upon a soldier than this journey to a delicate
woman," she commented.[8]

Nevertheless, she wrote, "I am all impatient to have our
building begun. ... I think it is very important for your
comfort, that your own house should be ready for you. ... a
crowded log house would not do for you."

As a postscript she added "tell Lucy (a younger sister) to
bring out a store of ink powder, quills and corset lace, and a
supply of good drawing paper, crayons and paints."[9] They
already were planning to open one of Leon County's earliest
schools.

So while the politics and social life of the wild new capital of
the Florida territory began to vibrate with duels and street
fights a dozen miles away, young Francis Eppes shrank from his

Plantation on Lake Lafayette

Sketch by de Castelnau in 1842 could have been Eppes' second plantation.

birthright of political activity and took up the hard life of making a beginning as a planter in virgin soil. A couple of times, later, he was called in to run local government in emergencies, but his primary involvement in community affairs was to help establish the Episcopal church, to campaign for establishment of a college in Tallahassee, and to exert his influence for law and order.

It may be that Francis Eppes couldn't have landed a major political job if he had wanted one.

By the time he settled at Tallahassee, most of the plums of territorial politics had been picked. Furthermore, the political star of the Virginia patriots—Washington, Jefferson, Madison, and Monroe—had set in the nation's capital, where Florida appointments originated.

The sun of Andrew Jackson, a comparative roughneck from Tennessee, was rising and his friends were getting jobs in Tallahassee. He had no reason to favor Francis Eppes, whose father had been a leader in the congressional investigation of Jackson's infamous execution of Ambrister and Arbuthnot at St. Marks a dozen years before.

As a committee held its hearings—27 days as tense as any during the scandals of our 20th century—Old Hickory paced the Capitol corridors threatening to cut off the ears of his critics.

At one point, according to Fuller in his book *The Purchase of Florida*, "Commodore Decatur with difficulty succeeded in preventing Jackson from entering the Senate Chamber to attack Mr. Eppes. Members of the committee went armed prepared to resist bodily assault with powder and bullets."[10]

That was Sen. John Wayles Eppes, Jeferson's son-in-law and father of Francis. He served four terms in the House and two years in the Senate from Virginia.[11]

Elizabeth Eppes died in Leon County after the birth of their sixth child. Francis sold L'Eau Noir, bought another plantation of 1,900 acres on Lake Lafayette, and also built a house at the southwest corner of Brevard and Monroe streets in Tallahassee.[12] His transformation from country planter to influential townsman followed.

Francis had epilepsy as a very young boy; but apparently he outgrew it, for there is no record of prolonged illness.[13] When he was eight years old, he went to Monticello to visit his grandfather, just out of the presidency. Jefferson reported to the boy's father that "Francis had enjoyed perfect and constant

health, and is as happy as the day is long. He has had little
success as yet with either his traps or bow and arrows. He is
now engaged in a literary contest with his cousin, Virginia, both
having begun to write together. As soon as he gets to z (being
now only at h) he promises to write you a letter."[14]

As an adult, he seems to have been of passive, though
resolute, character.

He was a scholarly man—well read in Greek, Latin, Spanish,
French and Italian, and the classics according to the instructions
of his grandfather and his schooling at the University of South
Carolina during his teens.

His education and family background made it natural that he
should be selected in 1833 by Gov. William P. Duval as a justice
of the peace—one of 14 in Leon County who handled minor
disputes and disturbances in their districts. He served six
years.[15] Duval, though a Kentuckian when appointed governor
of Florida, was the son of a revolutionary officer and Richmond
lawyer who was a close friend of Jefferson. The elder Duval had
been executor of the will of the murdered George Wythe, a
signer of the Declaration of Independence under whom Thomas
Jefferson studied law. Wythe became America's first college of
law professor, and was a mentor of John Marshall, James
Madison, James Monroe, and Henry Clay. So the Eppes-
Randolph family background surely was favorably known to
Duval before young Francis arrived in Leon County.[16]

Eppes married his second wife, Susan Margaret Ware,
daughter of Gov. Nathaniel Ware of Georgia, in 1837.[17]

While maintaining his successful plantation on Lake Lafayette, he began to take more and more part in civic affairs of his
town. Perhaps he was influenced by a letter his grandfather
Jefferson had written to him when he was 15:

"While you endeavor, by a good store of learning, to prepare
yourself to become a useful and distinguished member of your
country, you must remember that this never can be without
uniting merit with your learning," Jefferson admonished his
grandson.

> Honesty, disinterestedness, and good nature are indispensable to
> procure the esteem and confidence of those with whom we live, and
> on whose esteem our happiness depends. Never suffer a thought to
> be harbored in your mind which you would not avow openly. When
> tempted to do anything in secret, ask yourself if you would do it in
> public; if you would not, be sure it is wrong.

Eppes home in Tallahassee was on southwest corner of Monroe and
Brevard streets.
Razed in 1940s

In little disputes with your companions, give way rather than insist on trifles, for their love and approbation of others will be worth more to you than the trifle in dispute. Above all things at all times, practice yourself in good humor; this of all human qualities, is the most amiable and endearing to society.[18]

Whether Francis Eppes fully adhered to these precepts of conduct, we can't discern. Certainly, though, his record indicates he grew in the esteem of his Tallahassee neighbors.

He was one of the founders of St. John's Episcopal church, which was the third congregation established in the territory (1829). He was one of the nine members who agreed to be "bound and responsible" for $500 each to help fund the first church building in 1838. He was a delegate to the convention that year during which the Florida Episcopal diocese was formed, and later was secretary of the diocese for many years.[19]

Tallahassee in the 20 years from its founding to statehood was typical frontier territory. Ruffians brawled; the gentry fought duels (though not always fatally). Housing was primitive. Schooling was short and scarce.

However, there were those who looked for better things. The Rev. Seneca Bragg, upon arriving in 1832 to become rector of St. John's, wrote "perhaps in no portion of the United States, recently settled, and of equal population, is there such an amount of intelligence, as in Middle Florida."[20]

Eppes was on the side of righteousness and culture.

He and his father-in-law, Thomas Eston Randolph, were among the 13 men who, signing themselves "Trustees of the University of Florida," petitioned Congress in April 1836 for establishment of a "seminary of learning" in the territory.[21] The campaign was fruitless then; but when the "Seminary West of the Suwannee" (now Florida State University) finally was established more than 20 years later, Eppes declined an offer to become its president, though he served on its board of trustees.

Law enforcement was lax. The new capital didn't even have a secure jail for the first dozen years of its existence. Murders were not uncommon and, in one scandalous case, unpunished.

The St. Joseph *Times* of Sept. 4, 1840, reported:

The papers at Tallahassee, more than confirmed by private reports, show a disturbed state of society in Leon County, partaking of a personal and party character much to be regretted by every citizen of the Territory. We can't see why the gentlemen of Leon County

cannot differ in politics as in other parts of the country without
permitting unfriendly feelings to disturb their social relations.
Violence and proscription are not the best tests of sincerity and
honesty of purpose. Argument and a temperate discussion of
principles are the only weapons of a patriot politician. Pistols, Bowie
Knives and Bludgeons may frighten slaves, but cannot intimidate
freemen. We cannot commend to the parties of Middle Florida,
better advice than that engraved on the escutcheon of the great State
of Georgia:—WISDOM, JUSTICE AND MODERATION.[22]

Gov. Robert Raymond Reid even pulled troops away from
fighting Indians to help keep order at Tallahassee late in
1840.[23]

Much of the trouble arose naturally in the cussedness of a
wide-open town and its horse race track in the vicinity of what
is now Lake Ella. Much came from bitter politics. Susan
Bradford Eppes wrote that her father-in-law's reluctance to
enter public affairs broke down in the face of this lawlessness
and the murder of Gen. Leigh Read by Willis Alston,[24] and the
earlier death of a close friend, John K. Campbell, in a duel.

Read had killed Alston's brother, Augustus, in a duel. The
family sent for brother Willis, who previously had slain the
State Treasurer of Georgia in the Capitol at Milledgeville. Willis
returned to Tallahassee, and in 1841 murdered General Read
with a shotgun blast near the corner of what now is Park and
Monroe streets. He fled to Texas, where he later was lynched
for killing a man who had recognized him as an outlaw.[25]

Such a situation seemed too much for a simple justice of the
peace.

Whether by candidacy or acclamation, Eppes became mayor
of Tallahassee (intendant was the title conferred) in 1841.[26]

Yellow fever swept the town that year, which a visiting New
Englander, John S. Tappan, found to be not altogether
unfortunate. He wrote to a friend in November 1841:

> A year ago you could not walk the streets (of Tallahassee) without
> being armed to the teeth. . . . Now it's different for during the last
> summer out of a population of 1600 inhabitants God has seen fit to
> take away 450 of them composing most all of the Gamblers and
> Blacklegs of the place.[27]

The plague didn't solve all the problems. The Leon County
grand jury, Frances Eppes foreman, reported to the court in
April, 1842.

> On our oaths, we present the Marion Race Course as a public
> nuisance, a hotbed of vice, intemperance gambling and profanity,

deserving the just censure of every lover of decency and good order.[28]

The track was closed in 1843 perhaps more from economic pressure than public censure.[29]

Anyway, the efforts of Eppes and fellow reformers, aided by the fever epidemic and a fire that swept away most of downtown in 1843, gradually brought about a cleanup of frontier Tallahassee—physically as well as morally.

Eppes was elected four times to one-year terms as intendant during this critical period. Bertram Groene in *Ante-Bellum Tallahassee* gives this résumé of his tenure:

> In April 1841, Eppes organized a compulsory night watch to see that this whole new series of ordinances directed at establishing law and order was carried out. The new ordinances included prohibition of loud, profane, or obscene language, or riotous and disorderly conduct. The fine was from $10 to $100 and jail sentences from one to five days if the fines were not paid. It was also unlawful to expose in public within the city limits books, pamphlets, signs, pictures, drawings, or prints that might excite scandal or disturb the peace. It was forbidden to make any publication by 'sound of drumbeat or trumpet,' or to fire any gun, pistol, rocket, cracker, squib, or any other fireworks within the city. All drunk persons were to be brought before the intendant and fined from $5 to $50 or sentenced to from one to five days in jail. The night watch, created at the same time as the new ordinances to implement their enforcement, was composed of four or more men and was to patrol the city in two shifts from 9 o'clock in the evening until 1 in the morning and from 1 o'clock until 5 the same morning.[30]

After destruction of the shanty-built downtown business section in the fire, Intendant Eppes and his council adopted ordinances requiring the masonry construction in the rebuilding of destroyed structures.

For his services, a grateful citizenry presented the Intendant with a silver pitcher, engraved:

F. Eppes Esq.,
Intendant of Tallahassee, 1841-42.
A token of Regard From His Fellow-citizens
for his untiring and successful services
In the promotion of virtue and
Good Order.[31]

It was small tribute for a grandson of the author of American independence, but Eppes hardly would have looked for more.

Eppes was intendant again in 1856 and 1857. In 1866 when conquering federal troops under Gen. John G. Foster controlled the capital, he served once more as mayor. He was financially flat. In firm belief in the Confederate cause, he had sold his Lake Lafayette plantation the year before the Civil War ended for Confederate money. The money was worthless; his slaves were freed. Nevertheless, he took his duties as mayor of the fallen capital as seriously as if he really were in charge.

His daughter-in-law, Susan Bradford Eppes, recalled this ancedote:

> The district was fortunate then, for General Foster was far more reasonable and kind than most of our conquerors. He mingled with our people socially and "a game of chance" was often indulged in. One Sunday morning as the mayor was hastening down Monroe Street, intent on trying to get through his duties before the hour for church services, he passed a certain point where a half-sash gave a partial view of the basement below, and his sharp eyes spied the commanding officer of the post and the 'merchant prince' of Tallahassee busily engaged in a game of poker. Down the stairs went the mayor. The door was locked and silence reigned within when he knocked; a hearty push with his broad shoulders forced the door and the game was at once at an end. The mayor's family were terribly alarmed when this became known, but their fears were groundless. Monday morning there was a knock at the Eppes' door and a servant brought in cards, General and Mrs. Foster. Poor Mrs. Eppes trembled with apprehension, but summoning her courage she received her guests in her usual gracious manner. What was her surprise when General Foster told her that he and his wife had come to congratulate her on having such a husband; and they both praised his courage, his sense of justice, and his fair-minded execution of the laws.[32]

In 1869, Eppes sold his Tallahassee home and all his belongings, paid off his debts, and moved to Orange County to start a new life as a citrus grower. He immediately set about organizing scattered Episcopalians of the Orlando area into a congregation for prayer. After 10 years of occasional services with Eppes as a lay reader, the church established St. Luke's Mission at Orlando—which later became the cathedral for the Diocese of South Florida. Eppes died May 30, 1881, in a humble house at his orange grove at the age of 80.[33]

It was a long way from Eppington, Monticello, and Poplar Forest plantations of his boyhood, but who can say he had not fulfilled the hopes of his grandfather Jefferson that he would "become a useful and distinguished" citizen with "the esteem and confidence of those with whom we live, and on whose esteem our happiness depends"?

Randolph Connection

You can hardly separate the Jefferson and Eppes families from the Randolphs, and you cannot discuss Randolph kinships without a wall-chart.

The first of Thomas Jefferson's kin to reach the Florida frontier was his son-in-law Thomas Mann Randolph, who was sent down from Washington in 1826 to survey the disputed boundary with Georgia. A moody, quarrelsome, often dissolute fellow, he was given to excessive drinking and occasional mental breakdowns. However, he had served several terms in Congress and one term as Governor of Virginia with a disreputable administration. His work on the Florida-Georgia boundary seems to have been satisfactory, though inconclusive—mainly through lack of cooperation from Georgia state officers.[34]

Thomas Mann Randolph didn't stay long in Florida. He went back to Virginia, and soon followed Jefferson to the grave. It was his son, Thomas Jefferson Randolph, Francis Eppes' first cousin, who took over administration of the former president's bankrupt estate and settled its debts partly from his own resources.[35]

It probably would be wrong to say young Francis Eppes had been lured to Florida by his uncle's borderland descriptions. They were not that close. Besides, there probably was little that Thomas Mann Randolph could tell to embellish the reports of rich lands which were bringing distressed Virginians by the caravans to the Tallahassee country.

It was not only the lure of new cheap land.

Thomas Eston Randolph, first cousin of Jefferson and patriarch of the Florida Randolphs, left Virginia and followed his son-in-law, Eppes, to Florida "because he felt that there was too much intermarriage among the leading families. . . . Four of the children of his uncle William Randolph married Randolphs, and he himself married a distant cousin" (Jane Cary Randolph).[36]

His efforts to break up the chain of intrafamily marriages were successful in the new territory. Though his eldest daughter Mary Elizabeth had married Eppes (who had Randolph blood) in Virginia, the five other children married outside the family in

Florida—and very well. Harriet married Dr. Lewis Willis, descendant of George Washington and brother of Princess Catherine Murat; Lucy married planter John Parkhill; Arthur married Laura Duval, daughter of Gov. William P. Duval; Dr. James Henry Randolph, married to Margaret Hayward, sired the Whitfield and Randolph families long prominent in Tallahassee affairs.[3][7]

Thomas Eston Randolph and his daughters operated one of Leon County's first schools. The elder Randolph himself had not arrived in Florida before the school plans were well laid. Harriet wrote to him on September 20, 1829, about prospects for the boarding school at their plantation, Ethelmere, in a house then being built near Eppes' L'Eau Noir:

> A week ago I sent a few lines in your name to the Tallahassee paper. In this I simply stated that we proposed to establish a school, designated the place and the time (1st Jan'ry next) & referred persons for further particulars to F. Eppes and L. D. Hackley— before the 1st of Jan'ry. We will advertise more fully, but for the present I think this is sufficient, & less expensive. A report had gained ground for some time in Tallahassee, that we had declined establishing a school altogether & the people consequently were very anxious to get Mrs. Gray—She was thinking seriously of it, but Doct. Willis, who appeared disposed to be very kind & friendly to us, took pains to contradict the report, & Mrs. Gray thereupon withdrew. Whether she will not resume her intention, when she finds we are fixed 11 miles from town, I cannot say, but at least we have the start of her. There are doubtless several reasons why it would have been more to our advantage to go at once to Tallahassee, but after weighing the advantages on both sides, it will be found we have chosen wisely. The simple fact that we could not get a town house large enough to accommodate us for less than $600 or 700 a year, settles the matter in my mind, & I doubt not, will in yours also. As we shall live very cheaply and roughly—using only corn meal, brown sugar & salt meat—we set the price of Board (including washing) at $100 for boys. . . . Tuition in the English branches will be at three prices—first class $40—2nd 30—3rd 20—music 50, French and Spanish 25 each, drawing 25. I had once set them lower, but on further consideration thought it better to be above than below. These terms, however, are low enough heaven knows. It seems to be the general opinion that we shall have a full school, but I do not build too much on that—we have been often disappointed before.— As we now have two strings to our bow, & are no longer quite dependent on the patronage of the liberal & enlightened public, I shall not give myself the least uneasiness as to our success. The

plantation is our sheet anchor, & all that is made in other ways is over & above.[38]

The school turned into one for girls, and Mrs. Gray was a competitor.

It didn't last long. Harriet died three years later, in 1832. Her father already had been appointed U.S. Marshal for the Middle District of Florida, in Aug. 1831.[39]

Joseph M. White, Florida's delegate to Congress, recommended him to President Andrew Jackson as "an intelligent and accomplished gentleman, a man of business and integrity and competent to discharge the duties of any office the government could confer. He was the intimate friend of Thomas Jefferson, married the sister of Governor Randolph, and his daughter married the grandson of Mr. Jefferson. This gentleman was universally esteemed in Virginia and his appointment would be gratifying to his numerous friends there as it will be to all parties in Florida . . ."

Then there was the note so current in political recommendations of the period:

"Mr. Randolph by the decay of trade and depreciation of property in Virginia needs such an office for his support—the patronage of the government could not be bestowed on a worthier man."[40]

He wore the marshal's badge until 1837, when he resigned "as a consequence of poor health."

NOTES

1. John Wayles Eppes lived in Jefferson's home at Philadelphia from 1791 through 1793 while "Jack" attended the University of Pennsylvania in that city. Jefferson's letters to Jack's parents indicate a warm affection toward the Eppes family as well as close supervision of the young man's studies. See Sarah N. Randolph, *The Domestic Life of Thomas Jefferson* (Monticello-Charlottesville, Virginia: Thomas Jefferson Memorial Foundation, 1947), pp. 155, 165, 180 (hereafter cited as Randolph, *Domestic Life*).

2. Eva Turner Clark, *Francis Eppes: His Ancestors and Decendants* (New York: Richard R. Smith, 1942), p. 265.

3. Jefferson left for France in 1783 leaving his two youngest children Maria (Polly) and Lucy Elizabeth with their maternal aunt, Mrs. Frances Eppes of Eppington. His eldest daughter Martha (Patsy), who was eleven, accompanied Jefferson. Lucy died from whooping-cough in the fall of 1784. Maria joined her father in Paris in the summer of 1787, stopping for a fortnight with the John Adams family at London. The usually stern Mrs. Adams adored beautiful little Polly and wept at their parting. Randolph, *Domestic Life*, pp. 43, 47, 73, 96.

4. Nathan Schachner, *Thomas Jefferson; A Biography,* 2 vols. (New York: Appleton-Century-Crofts, Inc., 1951), 2:978.

5. Mary Elizabeth Randolph Eppes to Mrs. Thomas Jefferson Randolph, April 27, 1827, John Chipman, "Florida Randolphs and Related Families," unpublished manuscript, Winchester, Massachusetts (hereafter cited as Chipman, "Florida Randolphs").

6. Bertram H. Groene, *Ante-Bellum Tallahassee* (Tallahassee: Florida Heritage Foundation, 1971), p. 44 (hereafter cited as Groene, *Tallahassee*).

7. Harriet Randolph to Mrs. Thomas Eston Randolph, June 19, 1829, Chipman, "Florida Randolphs."

8. Ibid.

9. Ibid.

10. Hubert Bruce Fuller, *The Purchase of Florida* (Cleveland: Burrows Bros., Co., 1906), p. 265.

11. *Biographical Directory of the American Congress 1774-1961* (Washington, D.C.: United States Government Printing Office, 1961), p. 864.

12. Mrs. Nicholas Ware Eppes, "Francis Eppes (1801-1881), Pioneer of Florida," *The Florida Historical Society Quarterly* (October, 1926): 96 (hereafter cited as Eppes, "Pioneer"). William S. Branch, *The Eppes—Shine Families of Orange County, Florida* (Orlando, Florida: Southland Printing, 1949), unnumbered (hereafter cited as Branch, *Eppes-Shine Families*). For a map showing the location of the Lake Lafayette plantation see the inside cover of Clifton Paisley, *From Cotton to Quail: An Agricultural Chronicle of Leon County, Florida 1860-1967* (Gainesville: University of Florida Press, 1968). Paisley says that Eppes was a good farmer, producing 200 bales of cotton on 950 acres. Ibid., p. 13.

13. Fawn M. Brodie, Thomas Jefferson: *An Intimate History* (New York: W. W. Norton, 1974), p. 378.

14. Thomas Jefferson to John Wayles Eppes, 1809, Randolph, *Domestic Life,* p. 284.

15. Clarence B. Carter, ed., *The Territorial Papers of the United States,* 27 vols. (Washington: United States Government Printing Office, 1956), 24:815 (hereafter cited as Carter, *Territorial Papers*).

16. Julian P. Boyd and W. Edwin Hemphill, *The Murder of George Wythe: Two Essays* (Williamsburg, Virginia: Institute of Early American History and Culture, 1955), p. 20.

17. Branch, *Eppes-Shine* Families, unnumbered.

18. Randolph, *Domestic Life,* p. 314.

19. Joseph D. Cushman, *A Goodly Heritage: The Episcopal Church in Florida 1821-1892* (Gainesville: University of Florida Press, 1965), pp. 10, 11, 17, 78 (hereafter cited as Cushman, *Episcopal Church*).

20. Ibid., p. 11.

21. Carter, *Territorial Papers,* 25:267.

22. Quoted in W. T. Cash, *Florida Becomes A State* (Tallahassee: Florida Centennial Commission, 1945), pp. 18-19 (hereafter cited as Cash, *Florida*).

23. Ibid., p. 19.

24. Eppes, "Pioneer", pp. 98-99.

25. *Florida Mirror,* March 29, 1879, Fernandina, Florida.

26. Groene, *Tallahassee,* p. 176.

27. Cash, *Florida*, p. 19.
28. Ibid., p. 17.
29. Dorothy Dodd, "Horse Racing in Middle Florida," *Apalachee* (1948-1950): 20-29.
30. Groene, *Tallahassee*, pp. 102-103.
31. Eppes, *"Pioneer"*, p. 100. The pitcher is at Brokaw-McDougall House, Tallahassee.
32. Ibid., pp. 100-101.
33. Cushman, *Episcopal Church*, p. 128. Branch, *Eppes–Shine Families*, unnumbered.
34. For an interesting account of T. M. Randolph see William H. Gaines, *Thomas Mann Randolph: Jefferson's Son-in-Law* (Kingsport, Tenn.: Louisiana State University Press, 1966).
35. Randolph, *Domestic Life*, pp. 350, 351.
36. Chipman, "Florida Randolphs."
37. Ibid.
38. Harriet Randolph to Thomas Eston Randolph, September 20, 1829, ibid. Dr. Willis became very friendly indeed. He married Harriet in 1831.
39. Carter, *Territorial Papers*, 24:544.
40. Ibid., pp. 543-544. The U. S. marshal in Florida was more of a clerical functionary of the court than an active law enforcement officer of the later western kind popularized by television. The Florida Territorial Council had given primary law enforcement duties to county sheriffs. The first U.S. marshals vigorously opposed this law, but Washington backed up the sheriffs in a political showdown between the U.S. marshal and the St. Johns County sheriff at St. Augustine. Ibid., 23:165-6, 427.

Chapter Three

Planter's Lament

The broad plantations of Middle Florida had barely been established when hard times once more hit the emigres from older states hopeful of restoring family fortunes.

There was trouble with the Indians, who resisted removal to western reservations. That brought a seven-year inconclusive war which drew off the manpower for service in the militia from 1835 to 1842.

At the same time, the national financial panic of 1837 flattened farm prices and credit in the territory. Its banks, only recently organized on flimsy financial structures, failed and left the people so mistrustful that the principal issue on whether to accept the proposed state Constitution of 1838 revolved around its stringent, almost prohibitive restrictions on banking operations. One clause even barred bank presidents and directors from election to the governorship or legislature until a year after severing their bank connections.

As if the financial crash and the rebellious Indians weren't enough, the years of 1840 and 1841 yielded poor cotton crops to draw the low prices.

Things got so bad the Legislative Council suspended taxes on land and slaves for fiscal 1840-41.[1]

So planters and other citizens were in a forlorn mood when they formed the Leon County grand jury which met in April of 1842. It went beyond the normal chore of criminal inquiry to deliver a lamentation on economic conditions, the distress of landowners, fear of uprising, chafing at the shifting of officials appointed from Washington and impatience over getting on with statehood for Florida.

24

Frances Eppes was foreman of the grand jury. He signed the presentment first. Since he was the scholar of the panel, it doesn't seem fanciful to surmise he wrote it. His familiarity with the Latin classics, his undoubted reverence for his grandfather's word skill seem to recall the intonation of Cicero's orations and the ringing rhetoric of the Declaration of Independence.

It paints a dark picture:

General Presentments of the Grand Jury
of Leon County

April Term, 1842.

The Grand Jury of Leon county in bringing their short but laborious session to a close, have to remark with pain upon the present calamitous condition of the country.

Excessive speculation, and the inordinate issues of local Banks, have here, as elsewhere, been followed by wide-spread ruin. The extent and degree of distress is indeed, when taken in connection with the failure of several successive crops, and the great depreciation in the value of cotton, almost without a parallel.

There is no money in the country. Fifteen hundred executions are said to have issued from our Courts within the last five months, and it is a well known fact that there is not in the country specie enough to pay on these the legal fees of the officers of the Court.—What, then, must be the sacrifice of property! Sales have already occurred in which, in ordinary times, the property sold would have proved more than sufficient to cover judgment and costs—and what has been the result?—The plaintiff in one of these cases, by way of illustration, received about one-thirtieth of his original claim, one-tenth of the entire amount of the sale; and the other nine-tenths were required to defray the costs of suit and collection.

But dreadful as this result appears, it is but the feeble commencement of the utter destruction that is speedily to follow. And is such a condition of affairs to be tolerated?—Are the people to sit tamely by, and behold one by one of their number stripped of their property—of their only means of subsistence? and for what? Their debts are not paid—their property is gone, and neither plaintiff nor defendant benefited by the sacrifice. Is there then no remedy?

The conciliating policy, the recommendatory measures of public meetings—partly from the inability of those entrusted with collections from abroad to grant the required indulgence, and partly from the rapacity of others—must entirely fail. The arm of the Legislature has, so far, been extended in vain. The present *stay law* is of small benefit, except to that class who did not greatly need its assistance. What, then, can be done?

The resort to force is ever to be deprecated—but the Grand Jury believe that a more vigorous exertion of the Legislative arm is loudly called for; and that unless active measures are taken to invoke its aid, a state of things may and must ensue which every law-abiding citizen would deeply deplore.

It is far better that the representatives of the people should interfere, and cover with the Legislative sanction a restraint alike wholesome and necessary to creditor and debtor, than that an open resort to violence should be allowed to ensue. Deeply impressed with the reality and importance of this conviction, and anxious to avert the scenes of bloodshed and ruin which threaten to overwhelm this community, the Grand Jury of Leon county earnestly recommend to their fellow citizens, and to the people of Florida generally, a memorial and petition to his Excellency the Governor of this Territory, and through him to their Delegate in Congress, setting forth in strong and respectful language the evils complained of, and urging upon them the importance and necessity of the immediate passage by Congress of an act authorizing the Governor of this Territory to convene, as soon as practicable, the Territorial Legislature, to take into consideration such measures for the relief of this people as it might be expedient to adopt in the present crisis: and the Grand Jury do hereby for themselves, and in behalf of their fellow citizens, respectfully and solemnly solicit the co-operation of the Governor of this Territory, and of their Delegate in Congress, in the procurement of said act.

The Grand Jury present as an evil growing out of Territorial dependence, the melancholy system of proscription that has prevailed on the part of the General Government in their relations with this Territory during the last four years, and as evinced in the repeated and unjust removal from office of Territorial officers distinguished alike for probity and ability. If the faithful discharge of the duties of an office is to be no longer a guarantee for its continuance, it is high time that the appointment should revert to the people of the Territory: and the Grand Jury do therefore seriously and solemnly recommend to their fellow citizens the adoption of measures, as soon as constitutionally practicable, for the organization of a State Government.

In connection with the present distress of the country, and as greatly aggravated by it, the Grand Jury consider it their duty to present the enormous multiplication of legal process in the prosecution of suits, as an *intolerable grievance*, and one that calls loudly for legislative amendment. As an evil of the same character, and requiring the same redress, the Grand Jury regard the practice of marshals and sheriffs, in sales under execution. The property sold is so infinitely divided by being distributed for sale on different days of the week and month, that no concourse and competition of bidders can ever be expected, and consequently the sacrifices must be great. The Grand Jury respectfully recommend to the Marshal, as an act of justice to all parties, to set apart some one day and period of the month, on which all sales of property shall hereafter be made; and that this practice be observed until the Legislature can act on the subject.

The Grand Jury deem it, also, their duty to call to the attention the Honorable Judge of the Superior Court, the entire insufficiency of the security on both of the present Marshal's bonds, as a matter deserving immediate and special notice. Nor does the inadequacy of these bonds apply only to the sureties.—The amount fixed by law, the first to the U.S., being a bond for $20,000, and the second to the Territory for $10,000, is utterly insufficient. A bond for 50,000, well secured, would scarcely afford a sufficient guarantee for the safety of the immense sums which, in the present condition of affairs, must in the process of collection, pass through this officers hands. The Grand Jury consider this an evil of the first magnitude, jeopardizing alike the rights of plaintiff and defendant; and when it is recollected that the Marshal of the adjoining district lately availed himself of the circumstance to withdraw from the United States with a large amount of the public money, too much importance cannot be attached to it. The Grand Jury consider it a solemn duty to direct the attention of the proper authorities to the subject, and through our Honorable Judge and our Delegate in Congress, to request a prompt redress of the grievance.

The Grand Jury also present, as a serious injury to the country, the delay of the General Government in the payment of its debts to the citizens of this Territory; and they respectfully request their Delegate in Congress to press upon that body the speedy liquidation of these claims; and they would further urge upon his attention the fact, that it will greatly tend to relieve the pressure and distress occasioned here by the almost total absence of a circulating medium, if these payments be made in the notes of specie paying Banks, specie or Treasury notes, instead of *checks upon remote Banks*.

Under the head of County Business—

The Grand Jury present as a matter worthy of censure and prosecution, the long-standing negligence and inattention of the Board Commissioners of this County, and they advise that, unless a material alteration takes place under the recently appointed Commissioners, that proceedings shall be instituted against them, by the District Attorney, at the Fall Term of this Court.

The Grand Jury have, in the course of their duty, inspected the County Jail, and report with much satisfaction, and as highly creditable to the Sheriff and Jailer, its comfortable and cleanly condition. They recommend to the County Court the removal of the sheet iron lining, as a perfect nuisance, occasioning ill-health, and

decay of the inner timbers; and they strenuously advise also the
speedy erection of a proper enclosure as a precaution of safety and
cleanliness.

In conclusion, the Grand Jury of Leon County, tender in behalf
of themselves and the community, to the Honorable Judge of the
Superior Court, their thanks for his able and eloquent charge, and
for his energetic enforcement of the laws. Their thanks are also due
to the District Attorney and Marshal and other officers of the Court,
for their uniform courtesy and attention. The Grand Jury request of
the Court that this their General Presentment, may be published in
the several papers of Tallahassee.

Francis Eppes, Foreman.	Henry Williams,
Joseph W. Lea,	R. B. Kerr,
J. F. C. Harley,	J. S. Russell,
John P. Billingsby,	B. F. Whitner,
John Miller,	J. W. Bannerman,
J. C. Montford,	Charles Alligood,
J. G. Padrick,	Jacob Stroman,
H. B. Bradford,	John S. Shepard,
Dan'l T. Lingo,	Jabez B. Bull,
J. Atkinson,	Tom Peter Chaires.[2]

Statehood came three years later, by an act of Congress
signed March 3, 1845. It had been delayed six years after
adoption of the first constitution by differences within Florida
and by Congress waiting for Iowa to be admitted simultaneously so the Union would gain one congressional delegation from a
non-slavery state to balance the count of Senators and
Representatives from Florida, a slavery state.

Gradually, with statehood and national economic recovery,
Middle Florida planters entered a 15-year era approaching the
good old days of their families' past and their dreams for the
future.

It lasted only until the outbreak of the Civil War in 1861.

NOTES

1. This summary of conditions in Middle Florida was taken from
Charlton W. Tebeau, *A History of Florida* (Coral Gables, Florida:
University of Miami Press, 1971), pp. 125-131.

2. Clarence E. Carter, ed., *The Territorial Papers of the United States*, 27
vols. (Washington: United States Government Printing Office, 1956),
26:473-476. To facilitate reading, the text has been broken into logical
paragraphs.

Chapter Four

Man in the Shade

George Walton, Jr., son of a signer of the Declaration of Independence, is the neglected man of Territorial Florida history. He was overshadowed by his distinguished ancestry and, even to the end of his life, by a daughter poets and politicians acclaimed as one of America's most enchanting women.

He actually ran the territory as No. 2 man in the government for months at a time in the critical formative days of transition from a Spanish province to American governance.

During her lifetime his daughter was credited with choosing the Indian name of Tallahassee to remain on the town which grew up in ancient Indian fields to become the capital of all Florida.

However, there is no record that the brilliant and charming Octavia ever saw Tallahassee. She stayed with her mother and grandmother in Pensacola when her father moved to the new capital as territorial secretary. He was second in command to Andrew Jackson, then to Gov. William P. Duval, who was so given to absenteeism that Congress passed an act requiring territorial governors to get presidential permission to leave their territories.[1] Before that, President James Monroe once had ordered Duval back to Florida from Kentucky.

George Walton, Sr., of Savannah was a leader of the American independence movement when it was of dubious popularity in his region. He went to Philadelphia and, along with fellow Georgians Button Gwinnett and Lyman Hall, signed the Declaration for Georgia. He was wounded in the seige of Savannah. Both he and his wife Dorothy sat out the rest of the revolution as British prisoners of war on a West Indies island.

29

After the revolution, they returned to Georgia and settled at Augusta, where George, Junior, was born about 1790.

The elder Walton became a planter, Chief Justice of Georgia, governor and U.S. Senator. He was on the welcoming committee when President Washington visited Augusta on his Southern tour in 1791. He died in 1805, while his namesake was a student at Princeton.[2]

Young George, by all accounts a bright young man of good humor and convivial conversation, completed his studies in 1809 and married a 17-year-old belle of Augusta who had been his childhood neighbor and sweetheart. She was Sarah Minge Walker, daughter of one of Georgia's most distinguished jurists. George practiced law and served six terms in the Georgia House of Representatives.[3]

Daughter Octavia was 10 years old, her brother Robert 7, when her father took the lure of politics in the new territory of Florida. He accepted appointment as secretary of West Florida on July 12, 1821 and arrived in Pensacola a month later to assume the position. He took over from Richard Keith Call, who had been serving as Gen. Andrew Jackson's choice.[4]

Though Jackson had preferred to keep Call and seemed miffed at President Monroe's disregard of his own recommendations, he soon began to lean on Walton. Walton for his part, became a faithful Jackson follower and urged the general to announce early for the presidency in 1824. There was an element of job security in this, for Walton feared Secretary of the Treasury William H. Crawford, a fellow Georgian and political opponent, would beat John Quincy Adams and oust him from his Florida position.[5]

Jackson, remember, stayed in Florida only three months. He left abruptly for Tennessee on October 8, 1821, after delegating all his civil, military and judicial powers as governor to Walton in West Florida and his counterpart, W. G. D. Worthington, in East Florida.[6] Both of them governed with uncertain authority —reporting sometimes to Jackson at Nashville, sometimes to Washington—until Jackson's resignation was accepted at the end of 1821. Walton was the closer to Jackson, who directed Worthington to refer matters to him through Walton.

It was not a comfortable role.

Walton wasn't told how much salary to expect. He complained to Secretary of State John Quincy Adams that he found it expensive to follow Jackson's brief example of hospitable

Frick Art Reference Library

Octavia Walton by Sully
International charmer named Tallahassee

from Historic Mobile Preservation Society Collection

George Walton, Jr.
son of a signer of the Declaration of Independence
was in charge of territorial Florida for long periods

from the Historic Mobile Preservation Society Collection

entertainment. He didn't know whether Jackson's designation of him as acting governor conferred also on him the role of Superintendent of Indian Affairs (and the Indians were getting impatient for treaty talk). He did the best he could to handle Jackson's disputes with former Spanish officials and his quarrels with Monroe appointees in the tough manner started, and prescribed, by Jackson.[7]

Even after Jackson resigned and Walton and Worthington were notified to carry on as acting governors, the situation was unsatisfactory. It was another four months before Duval was appointed governor on April 17, 1822 to succeed Jackson. Two months later Walton wrote to Secretary of State John Quincy Adams, asking that he convey to the President his thanks for appointing him secretary of the whole territory under the Duval administration. But he was not happy:

> With the exception of Mr. Overton, one of the Commissioners, and Dr. Bronaugh, none of the gentlemen appointed to Offices in the Territory have arrived here—Governor Duval has not been heard from since he was seen by Dr. Bronaugh in Kentucky, but we are in daily expectation of seeing him. Last Monday the four members of the Council who reside at this place, (but who have not yet received their Commissions,) met according to the provision of the Act of Congress, and adjourned until the Monday following. What prospect there is of the arrival of the Members from St. Augustine I am unable to say. My situation at present is extremely unpleasant. An Opinion prevails among many that the temporary organization under General Jackson expired of itself with the end of the last Session of Congress, and that no legal Government can exist, until the one provided by the last Act of Congress shall be put in operation. For my own part I entertain no doubt that until the present government, be actually and practically superceded, it is my duty to proceed as heretofore—A different determination would lead to results from which the mind would revolt. Under existing circumstances I have endeavoured to do the best in my power. But in this state of uncertainty, almost all public business is at a stand, and some embarrassment has been Occasioned.

> I have not yet received any intimation from the Department of State of the amount which would be allowed me for my services as Secretary and Acting Governor of West Florida. This is at the present moment peculiarly desirable to me in order that I may be enabled to make arrangements which may be important to my private affairs.—

> I drew upon your Department on the 8th of October for three hundred dollars, on the 12th of November for four hundred dollars,

and on the 13th of May for five hundred dollars—Not knowing the exact sum I may expect to be allowed me, I have refrained from drawing for a greater amount until I should be informed on the subject.

I beg leave to call your attention to my letter of the 4th of December last on the subject of the rent of the house which I at present occupy, and the extra expenses I have unavoidably incurred, and most earnestly request that it be laid before the President for his consideration, if the subject has not already been settled.[8]

Duval arrived five days later; but Walton's burdens were not lightened.

Duval moved into the Walton home, along with Dr. Bronaugh. It must have crowded the Walton family which already was imposed on by having one room assigned to the father for an office.

There is no record of complaint from the hospitable Waltons to the extra company; but the Secretary did want some compensation. He wrote to Fontaine Maury, disbursing agent in the State Department at Washington:

I have left blank the charge for extra services rendered, and expenses incurred by me while Acting Governor of this Province. In several of my letters to Mr. Adams, I have taken occasion to explain myself on this subject. I throw myself entirely upon the justice and liberality of the President. When it is considered that my situation of Acting Governor was materially different from that of Secretary, I flatter myself that my claim will not be considered as unreasonable. As Acting Governor I was unavoidably compelled to see many strangers, and it was but decent, and proper, that some civilities should be shewn them. My actual expenses were at least treble what they would have been, had I continued to exercise only the Office of Secretary. The expense of living is even greater here than at New Orleans; and besides, the example of General Jackson, who was remarkable for hospitality, rendered it almost impossible for me to pursue a course entirely different, without giving offence, and even without lessening the respect for the Station, at a period when many circumstances combined to render it necessary that it should be maintained. I have observed the strictest economy in every thing which might become a charge on the Government; instead of renting an Office distinct from the House in which I live, I have made one of the rooms in it serve the purpose, not a little to the inconvenience of my family.

In addition to what I have just mentioned, I trust the President will take into consideration the various and troublesome duties which were devolved upon me, (according to the existing Spanish

Laws and usages) while in the exercise of the Government—Upon the whole I feel confident the President will be of opinion that an allowance for extra services, while exercising the Government, is but reasonable.[9]

Just as the Legislative Council began its first session, 57 days late, at Pensacola, yellow fever struck. Duval reported to the President:

It is with deep sorrow that I announce to you the death of my friends Doct. Bronaugh and Mr. Harrison, late Attorney for the United States on the 10th of August the yellow fever commenced in Pensacola with dreadful distruction—Very few of the great number that have been taken down, have recovered—Capt. Simms from Alexandria is also dead, I believe he held the appointment of Navy agent at Pensacola.

The best and most intelligent part of our American population has already fallen victims of this distructive fever—No hope is entertained of its abatement untill frost, which will not commence untill the last of October.

I lived with my friend Doct. Bronaugh in Col. Waltons family, It is almost a wonder that I escaped—for every member of his family has been or is now down with the fever except himself and his venerable mother I fear he will take the fever, and expect every day to hear this distressing intelligence.

The Spanish inhabitants stand it much better than our own people—not that they are exempt, for many of them have been, and now are sick—but few have yet died. . .

The distresses occasioned in Pensacola by the fever cannot be discribed, poor little children, without parents or friends are thrown on the charity of strangers we have not a cent to relieve the wretched The Spanish citizens act nobley, they have done and continue to do all in their power to relieve the sick Americans many of whom are taken to houses and nursed with the utmost kindness.

I have no funds either to pay the expenses incident to the sitting of the Legislative Council or to pay for the printing of the Laws of the Territory—altho, the act of Congress directs me to publish them, Is their no funds that can be used for these Objects I have written several times to Mr. Adams on these subjects but as yet have received no answer.[10]

Governor Duval wrote that letter on September 10, 1822. Before the end of the month he was off for his home in Bardstown, Kentucky.

He notified the Secretary of State on September 25:

I shall leave this (place) in a day or two for Kentucky and you will therefore address your communications to Col Walton, as Acting Governor.[11]

He didn't return to Pensacola until March 16, 1823—six months after he left Florida and four months after John Quincy Adams had written to him that "Some dissatisfaction having been excited by your absence, from the Territory of Florida I have been directed by the President of the United States, to inform you of his wish that you should return to it, with all convenient dispatch."[1][2] For one thing, Adams said, the Governor had to personally swear in a district judge for East Florida.

While Duval was away from Florida, Walton was having his doubts and his Indian troubles. He wrote to the Secretary of War:

> Upon the subject of Indian affairs, and particularly the treaty contemplated with those Tribes which reside in Florida, and to which your last communications relate, I have felt great solicitude, and exceedingly regret the absence of the Governor, of which, I presume, e'er this, you have been advised. I confess, that I do not see, in a manner satisfactory to my own mind, the relation in which the Secretary of the Territory stands to the Governor, as ex officio Superintendant of Indian affairs; neither do I understand clearly, the extent of my powers on this head, as acting Governor under the law of Congress. Notwithstanding this doubt, I should consider it my duty to act, if there were anything which the public service required to be done, and which might be in my power to accomplish; but upon this subject, I am entirely without means or instructions.
>
> It is unnecessary to state to you the situation of things in this section of Florida, in consequence of the dreadful pestilence which has prevailed in Pensacola. The sickness of my family, and of an esteemed friend (Dr. Bronaugh) who was confined at my house, detained me a considerable time, in the city, after the Legislative Council adjourned to Emanuel's. As soon as it was in my power to leave Pensacola, I was compelled to provide a shelter for my family in the woods, to which their safety urged me to retire; and therefore, saw but little of Governor Duval, previous to his departure for the state of Kentucky. Having made no communications to me on the subject of the Indians, all the information I possess in relation to it, has been gathered from the documents and papers left in my charge by the Governor, upon his leaving the territory, and the communications from your Department by the last mail, the receipt of which has already been acknowledged.— . . .
>
> Here I am at a loss to know, whether, in pursuance of the suggestion of Governor Duval, the Government has determined on holding no treaty, and if otherwise, whether Capt. Bell, or some other person has received instructions to proceed to St. Marks, and

accomplish the objects of the negociation. Unless the commissioner has been appointed, there will be no person authorized to meet the Indians in Council, and their assembling, must consequently, be productive of no valuable purpose. It was too late, even at the time of the Governor's departure from the Territory, to send word to the Indians, requesting them not to assemble, and giving the necessary explanations; and besides, I felt myself restrained from the adoption of this measure, by the letter of Governor Duval, of the 22nd of September, in which he says:—'I shall, however, direct the Indians to be assembled according to your desire; but hope that no treaty will be held with them, until this subject is further investigated.'

... Should I receive no further advices from the War Department upon this subject, and an agent should not be appointed to meet the Indians in Council, there does not appear to be any thing in my power, except dispatching a messenger to St. Marks, with letters to the Commandant of the place, informing him of the state of things which has unfortunately grown out of the circumstances already detailed. Without any authority to act as a Commissioner in holding a treaty with the Indians, myself, it would be useless for me to go to St. Marks. In the absence of the Governor, my public duties forbid it. My want of funds, also renders it impossible for me to make any preparations for supplying the Indians, who will probably, assemble at St. Marks in great numbers. They will, no doubt, be greatly disappointed, and in exciting a spirit of hostility, or interfere with any future effort at negociation, I cannot certainly anticipate. Upon an explanation to the Chiefs and Warriors, it is to be hoped that any difficulty will be obviated. . .[13]

Duval got back to Florida in time to, as he put it in his letter to the President, "place things on a proper footing at Pensacola."[14] Then he went to St. Augustine, where the legislature was about to hold its second session.

Walton couldn't go with him. He and his daughter, the precocious Octavia, were ill; and family obligations held him in Pensacola. Again, he complained to Washington about the uncertainties of his finances and his position.

In the course of a few days, I shall set out on my journey to St. Augustine, where the next Legislative Council is to be convened. I had intended to travil in company with Governor Duval, who left this [place] about two weeks since for East Florida; but have been unavoidably detained by my own illness and that of my family. At present, we are all upon the recover; and I am in hopes to be enabled to take my departure from Pensacola on Saturday next—

The serious inconvenience and expence to which I am exposed, in consequence of the seat of Government for this Territory not being permanently located, will be readily suggested upon the least reflection. I am compelled to be some time separated, at a considerable distance from my family, and to meet disbursements which will almost absorb the whole of my salary. It is very desirable that these difficulties should be obviated as speedily as practicable, and relieve me, as well as others from the embarrassments which they have created. Were the seat of Government permanently fixed, either in East or West Florida, or at a central position, equally convenient to both sections of Territory, it would be perfectly immaterial, so far as my individual interests are involved; but until this is accomplished, I cannot remove my family from Pensacola, with any confident assurances that they will remain for more than one year in a different portion of Florida.[15]

When Walton finally arrived in St. Augustine, Duval left the legislature in session and returned to Pensacola.

Soon after Tallahassee was established as the Capital in April 1824, Secretary Walton moved there with the records of government. Tradition has it that young Octavia, a linguist in her early teens who helped him with translation of Spanish documents, was influenial in giving the new capital village its old Indian name.[16]

He never moved his family to the village of log buildings, although the Tallahassee census of 1825 shows him as a resident with 17 slaves.

At Tallahassee, Walton was in charge much of the time. Letters from Washington were addressed to him almost as often as "lieutenant governor" or "acting governor" as they were by his proper title of "secretary." Governor Duval frequently found business to conduct elsewhere.[17]

Walton was on hand for the first sale of public lands around the quarter section reserved for the capital and it was Walton who selected the adjoining three quarter sections to the west and north for the city of Tallahassee. The first auction didn't bring in as much money as was expected. Some blamed heavy rains which left roads too muddy to travel just before the sale. Others blamed a late order from the Secretary of the Treasury refusing to accept specie issued by Georgia and South Carolina banks in payment for land purchased.[18] Of course, political shenanigan was hinted by critics of this directive; but Georgia and South Carolina banks weren't too solid at the time. Nevertheless, there seemed to be a good bit of Georgia and South Carolina money in the territory that couldn't be used to buy land.

As Secretary of State and acting Governor, Walton soon began to catch criticism from both ends of the old territory of Florida.

From St. Augustine, Customs Collector John Rodman was relentless. He was a man of chronic suspicion, who had had some private difficulties while U.S. District Attorney in New York City. He kept a steady stream of critical correspondence going between Florida and Washington.[19] Much of it was directed at Walton.

Rodman complained the politicians at Tallahassee were neglecting East Florida and the Indian menace in that region.

"Neither the Governor, nor the secretary who acts for him, during his absence, has been in this part of the Territory since the Autumn of the year 1823," he wrote to the Secretary of War on July 11, 1826, " and it is presumable they are entirely ignorant of the real State of affairs in this district. The Governor himself was absent from the Territory for upwards of a year in 1824 and 1825."[20]

Rodman complained also about the road which had been hacked out of the forest from St. Augustine to Pensacola—one of the nation's first roads to be built with federal financing. He said some stumps were left too high, at the eastern end, for wagons and carriages to clear them.

Worse than that, however, were his allegations that Secretary Walton was guilty of a conflict of interest by taking fees as official auctioneer for the sale of salvage from ships wrecked on the Florida keys.[21]

Actually, Rodman charged and no denial appears, the auctions were conducted by a Key West man acting as Walton's agent—and Walton wasn't on hand. Rodman, as collector at St. Augustine may have wanted those fees himself, since Key West was in the East Florida court jurisdiction. Key Westers, for their part, complained that St. Augustine officials were keeping them from having a court of their own in order to hold business for St. Augustine lawyers.

Rodman went so far as to charge that much smuggling to evade customs was being carried on through Key West and slaves were being illegally landed somewhere between Tampa Bay and St. Marks. "The father of one of the persons presumed to be engaged in this affair, resides near Tallahassee and is well calculated to afford every facility to the enterprise," he said in a letter to the Secretary of the Treasury dated June 10, 1826.

"Indeed I doubt whether a single individual could be found at Tallahassee who would throw any obstacle in the way of its accomplishment, afterwards or aid in the detention of the offence."[2][2]

The attacks on Walton from his own hometown Pensacola, were more serious. The *Pensacola Gazette* published rumors in 1826 that Walton had absconded with government funds. The editor demanded an investigation by the Legislative Council. There was a deficit in Walton's accounts, and his personal finances were in a shambles. He went to Washington, New York, Philadelphia and Baltimore in an unsuccessful effort to raise money to cover the shortage.[2][3]

He resigned as Secretary on December 14, 1826. Federal auditors found no serious fault with his handling of public money. There had been a mixup in adjustment of payments and settlements of accounts with Duval.[2][4] Walton owed the government $1,907.93, and he claimed the government owned him back salary and other amounts for extra expenses incurred while acting governor.

Walton went home to Pensacola and practiced law. He regained enough of his reputation to be elected to two terms in the Territorial legislature, but his enemies and financial troubles kept bedeviling him. He lost some of the blithe joviality which had been a hallmark of his personality. In 1829 he challenged one of his more relentless critics to a duel with pistols. Walton was hit and severely wounded.

He had saved his honor, but he may have begun to lose his family by a seven-year venture in early Florida politics which always seemed to show he was not measuring up to his illustrious father—the Signer, chief justice, governor, U.S. Senator. He moved to Mobile and became its mayor for two years; but by that time the Walton ladies were beginning to put George, Jr., in the shade.

Through all his experience as second man in rough and tumble pioneer politics, Walton's mother, Dorothy, and his wife, Sarah, had stayed in Pensacola doting over daughter Octavia as she grew into an early blooming charmer of young naval officers on duty there.

Octavia's first introduction to drawing room society was at the age of 14 when she represented her grandmother at a Mobile reception for LaFayette and delighted him with her adept conversation in French.[2 5] It was only one of her languages. She became famous for being able to carry on a conversation with several Europeans at a time, each in his own tongue. She had learned well and quickly from her private tutors not only a facility in foreign languages, but a fine taste for literature and a keen grasp of what was going on in politics.

Octavia is described as a graceful and dazzling beauty who had "acquired the Latin characteristics of speech—facial animosity, and tossing of the head, and eloquent gestures."[2 6]

She was no empty-headed coquette, though. It took more than feminine wiles to win the friendship and the extravagant praise she did from such disparate personalities as Edgar Allen Poe, Henry Clay, Washington Irving, John C. Calhoun and the French poet-statesman, Alphonse de Lamartine.

Before the family moved to Mobile in 1835, Sarah Walton inherited a small fortune from her father. She appears to have despaired of her husband attaining the station to which she aspired. He transferred his own charm and wit to the more pleasant company of drinking and political cronies. His mother, too, cut him off in her will, leaving what little she had to his children, Octavia and Robert. A year after Dorothy Walton died and was buried at Pensacola, her son's wife took her own patrimony and the two children for a long cherished social tour of the North.

Octavia was introduced to Washington society with a debut sponsored by Sen. Clement Clay of Alabama, whose wife was a relative of Sarah Walton. Octavia was socially triumphant in the nation's capital, but she didn't neglect the politics. She went often to the galleries to listen to great debates between Clay, Webster and other oratorical giants of the day. She could talk politics with them, as well as dance with them.

Years later, during her career as a lecturer and writer, she wrote and delivered an eloquent address at the laying of a cornerstone of a monument to Henry Clay at New Orleans.

Washington conquered, Sarah took Octavia on the grand circuit for social debuts in Baltimore, Richmond, New York, Boston, Newport and Saratoga. Her social success became a whirlwind.

She met Washington Irving on a stage coach. They became firm friends, and she was inspired to sharpen her own writing talents. She wrote and published articles, and at least one book,

"Souvenirs of Travel," published in 1857. Edgar Allen Poe, at Baltimore, wrote in her album:

> When wit, and wine, and friends have met
> And laughter crowns the festive hour
> In vain I struggle to forget.
> Still does my heart confess thy power
>   And fondly turn to thee.
> But Octavia do not strive to rob
> My heart, of all that soothes its pain
> The mournful hope that every throb
> Will make it break for thee![27]

Octavia and Sarah came back to Pensacola from that tour, then moved on to Mobile. There Octavia married a prominent young doctor, Henry LeVert, whose father had come from France with LaFayette to fight in the American revolution and was present with Rochambeau when the British surrendered at Yorktown.

The LeVert home in Mobile became such a popular attraction for the wise and the witty from at home and afar that she held a reception every Monday from 11 a.m. to 11 p.m. "Oakleigh," still a showplace in Mobile, was a magnet for writers, statesmen, actors and merchants of two continents.

Octavia took Europe the way she had American society. British aristocracy was abuzz when Queen Victoria invited her to a state ball before she had been formally presented. She appeared at the Court of Napoleon III in Paris.

"The most charming woman in the world," was the way the chapter on Octavia Walton LeVert started in the book, "Queens of American Society," published in 1867.[28] It quotes Washington Irving: "She is such a woman as occurs but once in the course of an empire."[29]

On many of her trips she was accompanied by her mother, Sarah and her daughter, Octavia II. Frequently, the author of Queens of American Society reported, "the mother, daughter and grand-daughter attend the same party, dance in the same quadrille, and attract their own separate coteries."[30]

The father, George Walton, Jr., became little known nor noted. He and Sarah were long separated. She stayed with friends when she was in Mobile.

The book *Women of the South Distinguished in Literature*, leads off with a chapter on Octavia, quoting extensively from her writings. It gives the father only passing mention about his experiences in Florida. Then he is dismissed: "He is now, at

Oakleigh
Home at Mobile which became a Southern mecca for statesmen and
intelligentsia attracted by Octavia Walton LeVert.
Now open as museum and headquarters of the Historic Mobile
Preservation Society.

sixty-nine, years of age, in vigorous health, and one of the raciest conversationists of the day."[3] [1] He died in Virginia and was buried there near the close of the Civil War.

NOTES

1. Clarence E. Carter, ed., *The Territorial Papers of the United States*, 27 vols. (Washington, D.C.: United States Government Printing Office, 1956), 22: 391. (hereafter cited as Carter, *Territorial Papers*). The restriction was removed the following year.

2. This summary of George Walton, Sr.'s career was compiled from *The National Cyclopaedia of American Biography* (New York: White & Co., 1898), 1: 219.

3. Leora M. Sutton, *The Walton House* (Pensacola, Florida: Pensacola Historic Preservation Society, 1968), p. 21 (hereafter cited as Sutton, *Walton House*).

4. Carter, *Territorial Papers*, 22: 43-44.

5. Ibid., pp. 298-299.

6. Ibid., p. 231.

7. Ibid., pp. 293, 299, 347, 481.

8. Ibid., pp. 456-457.

9. Ibid., pp. 481-482.

10. Ibid., pp. 531-532.

11. Ibid., p. 538.

12. Ibid., p. 563.

13. Ibid., pp. 557-559.

14. Ibid., p. 649.

15. Ibid., pp. 665-666.

16. Mrs. E. Fries Ellet, *Queens of American Society* (Philadelphia: Porter and Coates, 1867), p. 400 (hereafter cited as *Ellet, Queens*).

17. Carter, *Territorial Papers*, 23: 242.

18. Bertram H. Groene, *Ante-Bellum Tallahassee* (Tallahassee: Florida Heritage Foundation, 1971), p. 22.

19. Carter, *Territorial Papers*, 22: 17.

20. Ibid., 23: 605.

21. Ibid., pp. 537-538.

22. Ibid., p. 590.

23. Sutton, *Walton House*, p. 31.

24. Carter, *Territorial Papers*, 23: 688.

25. Sutton, *Walton House*, p. 30.

26. Ibid., p. 31.

27. Ibid.

28. *Ellet, Queens*, p. 396.

29. Ibid.

30. Ibid., p. 414.

31. Mary Forest, *Women of the South Distinguished in Literature* (New York: Derby and Jackson, 1861), p. 16.

Chapter Five

William Wirt's Dream

One of the great lawyers of early American history started a plantation between Tallahassee and Monticello with contracted free white labor during the hey day of slavery, but the project collapsed when the free workers ran out on their contract.

William Wirt, Attorney General of the United States in the Monroe and John Quincy Adams administrations, wanted to spend his declining years in Middle Florida. It was a dream that has been shared by many over the years.

Wirt was born in Maryland in 1772 of Swiss and German parents.[1] He was one of the prosecutors of Aaron Burr for treason in 1807, attorney for the Cherokee Nation in its effort to resist being removed from its native Georgia territory in 1830, and a candidate for the presidency in 1832.[2] He opposed Daniel Webster in the famous Dartmouth College case and won from Webster an observation that Wirt "is a good deal of a lawyer, and has very quick perceptions, and handsome power of argument."[3] He was an intimate friend of such men as Thomas Jefferson, and evidently shared Jefferson's objections to slavery, on principle. He was author of an early biography of Patrick Henry, a work with which Jefferson helped him.[4]

As early as 1825, only four years after the Territory of Florida was acquired by the United States from Spain, Wirt began making his plans for a life of leisure and luxury in the Tallahassee area.

Earliest entry found on the land records of Jefferson county is in the name of Elizabeth Gamble Wirt, his wife. About three miles southwest of Monticello, the land described in the April 23, 1825, entry was the eventual site of Wirtland plantation, but its establishment didn't follow William Wirt's new and visionary plan.

Wirt's enthusiasm for Florida living—though he may never have come to the state—was so great that he bought enough land in the area to give each of his children a plantation.

Laura Henrietta, born in 1803, the oldest of 12 Wirt children, was the first to be given Florida acreage by her father.

During the summer of 1827, Laura Wirt married Thomas Randall of Annapolis, Md., who was then an attorney in Washington. His father-in-law, in his second term as Attorney General, perhaps had a hand in Randall's prompt appointment as a District Judge in the New Territory.[5]

The young couple, accompanied by Mrs. Wirt's two brothers, John and Robert Gamble (briefly secretary to John Marshall) and their families, who also had visions of fortune and good living in North Florida, arrived in Leon County during the fall of 1827.[6]

The Randalls immediately began establishment of Belmont plantation, in the same area as the first Wirt land purchase. The Gambles too, started plantations with high hopes for the future.

Advice to his daughter in 1827 is contained in a letter from William Wirt to Laura Wirt Randall:

> Will you let me give you a hint? You are going to a newly settled country—do you wish to make your husband and yourself popular? Dress as plainly as possible, and conform as closely as you can to the manners of the place. Any other course, especially fine dressing and haut-ton manners will excite only envy, criticism, malignity, quarrels and contempt.[7]

A note of cheer to a homesick daughter, resident of the Territory of Florida for several months, U.S. Atty. Gen. William Wirt, December, 1827:

> I think you will do well,—and I am so much delighted with every report that reaches me of the country, that I count sanguinely myself on settling a plantation and coming out to live. I have none of your horrors of a country life in a new country. Florida bids fair to be a perfect Arcadia. Such a climate! Such a soil! Such productions and such society as you will have in a few years! Can anything be more delightful!
>
> How dull and monotonous Washington is, as compared with the new objects that are continually meeting your eye!—the fine forests, the fine lands, the balmy, gental air, the tropical-tinted birds, the alligators, the barking frogs, and all the other elegancies of nature's drawing room. You must not despond, my dear child.[8]

In a letter to William Pope in March 1828, Wirt said, "I suppose you saw Governor D—-, on his way through Virginia. He is a lighthearted, joyous fellow, and has gone home buoyant with the hope of fortune by the culture of sugar and sea-island cotton. They are all sanguine on this subject in Florida,—and I think they have reason. But we have yet to see what lesson experience will teach. My two brothers and my son-in-law have turned into cropping might and main—and I dare say they all count upon being rich in ten years . . . ."[9]

Experience taught the Randalls and the Gambles the slave-worked plantations in Florida could indeed succeed, as they were succeeding all over the rest of the South.

But William Wirt and another son-in-law had a different plan.

It was carefully thought-out. It was designed for the comfort and contentment of German immigrants under contract as laborers, and as an eventual "princely establishment" and "comfortable asylum" for members of the Wirt family and German colonists alike.

Louis Goldsborough, Lieutenant in the Navy, was the new husband of Elizabeth Wirt, second daugher of the house, and a man of imagination. His scheme for the establishment of Wirtland was new and visionary in 1833, but practical men thought it would succeed.

In a letter to Mrs. Wirt, written from Washington on January 31, 1833, Wirt explained the plan to her:

—Here I am waiting—, meantime helping Louis with his whaling project, as he calls this German scheme. The whaling voyages, he says, suggested it to him. The only pay the sailor gets in these voyages is what they call 'lay'; that is, a share of the profits. And yet they are the happiest and most faithful of seamen. I have been so often baffled in my attempts to settle our Florida tract, that I expect the same disappointment in this attempt. Yet Louis and his other friends are so sanguine that I begin to suppose the thing may be possible.

I offer to take them out at my own expense, support them till the plantation will maintain them—to buy cattle, hogs, sheep, etc.,—to find horses, mules, and all the utensils necessary to the plantation, and to give them one-third of the clear profits.

They are to go with Louis to be placed under his government and direction. Their preacher, a Calvinist, will accompany them, and be the schoolmaster for their children. They will form a fine little village in the settlement, with their gardens in the rear of their dwellings, a broad street between, and a church, schoolhouse and

William Wirt
(1772-1834)
Twice U.S. Attorney
General, owned plantation,
Wirtland, between
Tallahassee and
Monticello

Louis Goldsborough
(1805-1877)
Wirt's son-in-law. His
free labor plantation
scheme failed, but he
rose to Admiral in the
U.S. Navy.

American Portrait Dictionary

parsonage at one end. In short, if they prove faithful and honest, it will be a thriving and happy establishment. And as they will be well educated, intelligent, moral and Christian, it will be, if Providence blesses the design, a most princely establishment for you and our children.

It is a part of the arrangement that there is not to be a black on the place. The project is new in our country, looks rather visionary, and very like one of the castles in the air; but practical men here think it must succeed.[10]

Goldsborough went ahead with arrangements in Baltimore for getting the project under way. Careful selection of colonists was possible because applicants "are pressing upon him (Goldsborough) so anxiously that he has no doubt he could get two boat loads in Baltimore alone; besides the importunities of Germans here, who follow him to Baltimore", Wirt wrote to Thomas Randall from Washington in mid-February.[11]

On March 22, the brig "Laurel" sailed for Florida with 150 people aboard, all of the same religion—protestant—and from the same German province, or the neighboring one of Bavaria. The adults were bound by covenant for five years, and the children until they were 21. Goldsborough always was to hold back their share of the profits for one year, which would be forfeited by "infidelity to their engagements."[12]

Further instructions for the general happiness and contentment of his labor force were sent by Wirt on March 30 to await Goldsborough's arrival in Tallahassee.

"When I learn you have got your colony to Wirtland, and that your Germans are busily and cheerfully engaged in building their village, I shall feel greatly relieved and comparatively secure," he wrote.[13]

Every cabin, with its garden and milch cow, will be a new anchor to wind ward. And when the church and school-house are built and their children are going to school, and their own pots boiling merrily, I shall consider them, and your project, safe in dry-dock. Let them have no complaint on the score of plenty and comfort, and I think all will go well.

Remember that our great object is to get as much clearing done by these Germans as possible the first year, so as to make sure of reimbursing ourselves the cost of their transportation and support. Push that object, therefore, as far as it can safely be pushed.

Meantime, I would suggest the propriety of doing everything for their recreation that can be done compatibly with industry. I would even promote their festivity and enjoyment. I would ask them to give me a specimen of the rustic waltz of Germany and encourage music, dancing and all innocent amusements. Let the boys play leap-frog, prison base and ball in the street, or court, between the houses of the village, for the entertainment of their parents. Set some of them, in their leisure, to making Alp-horns for your shepherds. All these things will serve to knit their hearts to the place by multiplying their local associations and strengthening their gregarious propensities to their own particular society. There is nothing so exhilarating as the song of healthful, cheerful industry; and I hope to hear your people are too happy to be disposed to separate, either from each other or from you.[14]

Goldsborough and his colonists arrived in Florida sometime before the end of April. Just how carefully laid plans proceeded at Wirtland for the first several months of the project is lost in the haze of the past, but it didn't turn out that the people were "too happy to be disposed to separate" from either Louis Goldsborough or their contracts.

In less than three months, they had separated themselves permanently from Wirtland, and William Wirt had been separated from the $6,000 to $8,000 that he estimated as the initial cost of the venture. Available records don't reveal where the Germans went, but apparently they left the Tallahassee area.

In a letter dated July 18, 1833 to Goldsborough, Wirt said:

With regard to the Germans, considering what kind of cattle they have proved to be, I am so far from lamenting their desertion, that I think it quite a happy riddance. Never mind the affair. It is only one of 'our castles' tumbled down. I am so used to such things that I am rather more disposed to laugh than to weep at them. Thank Heaven, there are no bones broke in the way of pecuniary loss! We had, at least the foresight to anticipate such a result, and to take care to make the experiment as cheaply as possible. I am sorry for your disappointment. But regrets are vain. The thing has been done. We must not be unnerved by the disappointment but provide as vigorously as we can to meet the future.[15]

To his other son-in-law, Thomas Randall, Wirt wrote:

—I wonder how Louis has been able to bear up under it. I am infinitely more sorry on his account than my own. I know how much he had it at heart, and how sanguinely he counted on success, which I never did. Without any pretensions to so high a character, I think I can assure you that this affair will not leave a scar on my brain or my heart. Indeed, the explosion has been so quick and so complete, and there is something so droll in those rascals having gone so far to play so ridiculous a caper, that it seems to me rather more laughable than cryable; and much the strongest tendency I feel is to laugh, until I remember Louis's disappointment and mortification.[16]

Failure of this cooperative approach to plantation development dimmed neither Wirt's enthusiasm nor his hopes for retirement in the Florida Territory. By December of 1833 he had another plan afoot, and expected to be living in Florida "after two winters more, if we all live so long."[17]

Unfortunately, William Wirt didn't live so long. He died on Feb. 18, 1834, shortly after receiving news of the death of his eldest daughter, Laura Wirt Randall, at Belmont plantation.[18] Judge Randall and his four young daughters later moved to Tallahassee and occupied the house still standing on the southwest corner of Calhoun and Carolina Streets.

Wirtland eventually was established for Mrs. Wirt and the remaining children by Louis Goldsborough, but with slave labor, in the manner of the times rather than with his earlier "new and visionary" plan. Goldsborough went back to his career in the Navy. He was head of the Naval Academy from 1853 to 1857, was made a Rear Admiral in 1862, and finally retired shortly after 1873.[19]

Wirtland was described in "Florida Breezes," Ellen Call Long's book of reminiscence of early days in this section of Florida:

> The dwelling at Wirtland was a plain but commodious country house, upon approaching which no noisy hounds assailed you, but a Negro major domo, and one or two neatly dressed Negroes, met the party at the gate, which, opened, we were ushered into a garden of trailing vines, luxuriant shrubbery, brought to view by a holocaust of pine knots, on which had been cast sweet spices, and the porch was crowded with floating muslins and ribbons. . . .
>
> Within there were white curtains looped with blue, and there were settees, ottomans, and chairs, all in blue and white. A conspicuous feature was a portrait of the distinguished orator (Wirt) represented in a Roman toga; but this retreat that he had provided for his declining years was scarcely planned before he was taken from his family and the nation; he never saw it, but his wife and daughters make it their home for the present. Mrs. Wirt is soft mannered and self poised, and wears a turban which adds the picturesque to her appearance, and eider-down cushions in her sleeves, that we still marvel over in the line of fashion. . . .
>
> The hennery was a neatly white washed latticed shed, down the centre of which were two or three tiers of shelves, divided

perpendicularly with boards, thus forming rows of nests one above the other; and these were curtained with colored calicoes of pink, blue and red, all neatly hemmed and finished. It was odd, but it was nice, thus to follow out the natural instincts of fowls to hide their occupation. . . .[20]

NOTES

1. John P. Kennedy, *Memoirs of the Life of William Wirt: Attorney General of the United States*, 2 vols. (Philadelphia: Lea and Blanchard, 1850), 1: 16 (hereafter cited as Kennedy, *Memoirs*).

2. Ibid., 1:152, 2:240, 2:303.

3. Fletcher Webster, ed., *The Private Correspondence of Daniel Webster*, 2 vols. (Boston: Little, Brown and Co., 1857), 1:275.

4. The publication of Wirt's book (*Sketches of the Life and Character of Patrick Henry*) coincided with his appointment as Attorney-General (1817). While generally favorably received, the biography was severely criticized by *The North American Review*, which was probably the most important American periodical of the era. Both Thomas Jefferson and John Adams praised the book, but had reservations. Jefferson pronounced portions of it "a little too poetical." Adams felt that Wirt's portrayal of Henry slighted the role of James Otis in the Revolution and subsequently (1819) published a series of political essays on the years 1774 and 1775. Kennedy Memoirs, 2: 24, 42, 43.

5. Ibid., 2:201.

6. Ibid., 2: 202.

7. Ibid., 2: 203.

8. Ibid., 2: 206.

9. Ibid., 2: 211.

10. Ibid., 2: 337.

11. Ibid., 2: 339.

12. Ibid., 2: 338.

13. Ibid., 2: 341.

14. Ibid., 2: 341-342.

15. Ibid., 2: 343-344.

16. Ibid., 2: 344.

17. Ibid., 2: 363.

18. Ibid., 2: 367.

19. Allen Johnson and Duman Malone, eds., *Dictionary of American Biography*, (N.Y.: Charles Scribners Sons, 1931), p. 366.

20. Ellen Call Long, *Florida Breezes: or Florida, New and Old* (Gainesville: University of Florida Press, 1962), pp. 130, 133.

Chapter Six

Log Cabin Royalty

Descendants of George Washington's immediate family arrived to settle in the new territorial capital of Florida the year after the site was selected.[1]

Besides the prestige associated with a close Washington connection, Byrd and Mary Willis brought with them a daughter who was to become one of territorial Tallahassee's most glamorous ladies, a princess by marriage to Napoleon's nephew, Achille Murat.

Catherine Daingerfield Willis was born in Fredericksburg, Virginia, on August 17, 1803. Her maternal great grandmother was Betty Washington Lewis, of Kenmore, sister of George Washington. The great grandmother on her father's side was George and Betty Washington's aunt, and, incidentally, George's godmother. Besides this, there was Washington kinship through her maternal grandfather. Her Washington connections were very good indeed.[2]

Catherine's mother was Mary Lewis, daughter of Major George Washington Lewis of Marmion. The plantation house at Marmion, in the Northern Neck of Virginia, is one of the oldest great 18th century houses still standing, and is famous for its fine paneling. The original woodwork of the drawing room, removed to the American Wing of the Metropolitan Museum, is one of the Museum's prize exhibits.

Catherine's father was Byrd Willis, of Willis Hill, now a part of Fredericksburg, Virginia.

Catherine's first husband was Atchison Gray. His father was wealthy John Gray, of "Travellers' Rest" on the Rappahannock River in Virginia. She was very young when she went with her

young husband to live in a small cottage at Wakefield
Plantation, George Washington's birthplace, where Atchison
Gray was superintendent. He lived less than a year after their
marriage, and the young widow went back to her family near
Fredericksburg.[3]

This was in 1821. By 1825, the Willis family fortune had
dwindled alarmingly, the house had burned, and Byrd Willis had
rented the inn in Fredericksburg as a home for his family of
eight children and a place to continue the lavish entertaining of
friends he enjoyed so much.

In memoirs that Byrd Willis started writing about 1827, in
Florida, he says of himself: "I was an idle fellow, fond of fox
hunting, racing, and convivial parties, paid no attention to
plantation business, and but for the profits of my race course
and the sale of firewood, would have run through the girths
long before I did. In 1825, finding that things were getting
worse and worse, I sold off, paid off, and came off, to this
Territory, Florida."[4]

The Willises settled in a small log house on Monroe Street,
and the widowed Catherine was soon a belle among the eligible
men of the brand new town.[5]

Among her admirers was Prince Charles Louis Napoleon
Achille Murat, nephew of Napoleon Bonaparte, and Crown
Prince of Naples until the downfall of the Emperor. The
Prince's father was Marshal Joachim Murat, of the Napoleonic
armies, and his mother was the Emperor's youngest sister,
Caroline. Caroline is said to have been a very beautiful and
ambitious woman, and wasn't completely happy with her
brother's Empire until he saw fit to make her Queen of Naples,
and her husband King.

Achille was the oldest of the four Murat children and, as
Crown Prince, was being educated for the throne until the
downfall of Uncle Napoleon. The great good fortune of the
Murat family came to a bitter end in 1815—King Joachim was
shot, the Queen and her children were exiled to a remote castle
in Austria.

By the winter of 1822-23, Achille had gained permission to
leave Europe for America, where his Uncle Joseph, former King
of Spain, had fled in 1815. Joseph established a princely estate
near Bordentown, New Jersey, and having gotten out of Europe
with a sizeable fortune, proceeded to live out his days in the

Achille Murat
Nephew of Napoleon
Bonaparte
eccentric Florida
planter

*Copy of portrait in
Walker Library,
Tallahassee*

Catherine Murat
From George Washington's
family was among
Florida capital's first
belles.

*Paintings by
Claribel B. Jett
for Murat House at
Tallahassee Junior
Museum*

general manner to which brother Napoleon had made him accustomed.

Achille Murat came to America very nearly empty-handed, but with visions of making a fortune of his own in short order.

The new Territory of Florida seemed to offer much in the get-rich-quick scheme he had planned for himself; so after a visit with Uncle Joseph and his cousins, and a trip to Washington to watch democratic government in operation, he started South. Charleston enchanted him, but Florida and a quick fortune had even more appeal.

He arrived in St. Augustine in April of 1824, and rented a small house still standing in the old part of the city and suitably marked as once his residence. At the end of two months, he had bought an estate of 1200 acres not far from town, and began experiments in planting cotton, tobacco, sugar cane, oranges and other tropical fruit. Later he bought a hundred head of cattle; but life in East Florida soon lost its attraction for him, and he left for newly-opened Middle Florida and the prospects of a quicker fortune, in October of 1825.[6]

A land partnership with Col. James Gadsden ended in the establishment of Achille Murat's first Middle Florida plantation, about 15 miles east of Tallahassee. He called it Lipona, in honor of his mother, who took the title of Countess of Lipona—an anagram of Napoli, or Naples, when she was stripped of her queenly title and forced into exile in Austria.[7]

There's a story that the Prince and Catherine met for the first time at a picnic at Fort San Luis, ruins of a Spanish mission which was old even then.[8]

During the afternoon, one of Catherine's slippers fell off. Achille seized it and drank wine from it—there are overtones of Cinderella here, but Kate, as she was called, was hardly the Cinderella type.[9]

She was a Virginia lady, descended from a long line of Virginia ladies. Mama would never have allowed Catherine to clean the hearth and polish the andirons and such, though she was most particular about her housekeeping.

Mrs. Willis took an especially bleak view of tobacco chewers and the havoc they wrought with her highly polished andirons and floor. The Prince was an inveterate chewer, but he cleverly solved the problem when calling on Catherine by taking along a shaggy dog to use as a spittoon.

It was to Lipona Plantation that Achille took Catherine Willis Gray when his successful courtship blossomed into marriage on July 12, 1826.[10] The residents of Middle Florida were enchanted with the marriage. One group whispered that Catherine had done very well, indeed, and who knew? She might one day sit on a throne. There was always the possibility that the Bonapartes would be restored to power in France.

Another group declared flatly that Napoleon's nephew was far from being the equal of so well-born a Virginian. The Bonapartes were of obscure Corsican ancestry of whom nobody had ever heard until a mere quarter of a century before. Royalty, indeed!

Catherine must have had a great liking for royal ways, as description of the house at Lipona Plantation plus some of the legends about her later life at Bellevue indicate.

According to Ellen Call Long, who, though younger, was a contemporary of the Princess Murat, there was a large square garden at Lipona, planted with orange shrubs, vines, vegetables and flowers. The parlor and dining room building, with its veranda was in the center. Around the four sides of this were log buildings, each one a single room. The logs were white-washed, and the pine window frames and shelves inside were covered and curtained with looped muslin and laces. The sheets and pillow cases in the bedroom buildings were linen and the towels were embroidered in silk with the crown and coat of arms of the King of Naples.[11]

Tea and coffee were served with golden teaspoons marked with Napoleon's crest. Napkins were damask, woven with the royal crest. There was a marble bust of Queen Caroline, done by Canova, an outstanding sculptor of the Napoleonic era.[12] Such elegant furnishings of rude cabins were neither unusual nor considered pretentious in territorial Florida. A letter from O.T. Hammond, a teacher, to a friend in New York, dated at Tallahassee in November, 1838, reveals some strange contrasts:

This is a cold night—mercury 33°— and our cabins are miserable things— Did I ever give you a hint of the Southern palaces—well here it is. I belive that my prison, for such it has been to me for most of the summer, is a fair specimen of our architecture. It is made of pine logs—I should have said poles—6 inches apart—the interval is partially closed by pine splints so thin that they are translucent—in many places I could almost throw a ball through. Our chimney is made of clay and sticks—not a brick or stone about the inside. . .

Bellevue
Tallahassee home of Catherine Murat
after death of Prince
Copy of an 1885 sketch
House has been moved to grounds of Tallahassee Junior Museum and
restored.

Bellevue interior restored, fine furnishings within unsealed walls.

Our bed curtains shiver like an aspen leaf—the candle flares—the wind whistles through a thousand breathing holes—you sit close to your roaring fire until your shins are well nigh blistered and then turn round to thaw your back.

A stranger is astonished at the strange incongruity he sees. A poor old crazy log hut is often splendidly furnished, pianos; sofas; mahogany tables; rich side-boards—Turkey carpets; cut glass;—If he attends church he sits upon a slab in a log cabin—not a window or door—a pulpit more like the fiddle box in our old school room than what he had associated with the name of pulpit. He does not see the same simplicity in dress, but the fair all clad in rustling silk—gold watches, gold pencils, gold scissors, gold quizzing glasses, and gold spectacles; nor will he see much want of splendor in the equipage gilt carriages; fine horses; servants livery; so much show.[13]

No doubt in deference to her husband, Catherine used the title Madame rather than Princess. He was so impressed with the American form of government that he insisted on being known as a plain citizen and used his Florida militia title of Colonel, instead of being known as a Prince.

Achille Murat liked life in this country, and was particularly intrigued with the flora and fauna of his new home.

He delighted in experimenting with native plants, and often confounded the cook by furtively introducing various wild herbs into her cooking. One afternoon while Catherine was visiting friends at a neighborhood plantation, Achille mixed a huge caldron of dye from wood and plants he had gathered; and when she came home he greeted her with "Oh, Kate, I have succeeded; I have made all your clothes a most beautiful pink".[14]

Calling on a friend at Lake Jackson one morning, the Prince found him shooting buzzards in a big oak tree. The friend remarked that this was the greatest country for wild turkey he had ever seen—that he often had them for his dinner.

According to contemporary sources, the Prince exclaimed, "Wild turkeys! Mon ami, . . . those are the buzzard, . . . but . . . cook him again today, for I will eat him." Later, he told friends, "I must confess that I found it tough, with some more objections."[15]

In spite of his appreciation of life in a republic, Colonel Murat kept a sharp eye on affairs in Europe, and at the drop of every favorable rumor, he and Catherine set sail, always in the hope of recovering their share of the Murat fortunes that had been confiscated at the end of the First Empire.[16]

They had no money. All they possessed was mortgaged to the hilt, but somehow, in those days of few if any banking laws, one bought land on credit, then borrowed money on the land to buy more land on which to borrow more money.

This is how they financed their trips to Europe and business ventures in new places—this plus a small allowance from Caroline Murat until her death in 1839. For payment of small debts, Murat printed his own scrip—bills worth 12-1/2 cents when traded with Tallahassee merchant E. Lookermann with whom he apparently carried an account.[17]

In the fall of 1835, the Murats abandoned Lipona Plantation to an overseer and went to New Orleans where Achille was sure he could make a fortune with his newly-acquired knowledge of law.

They bought a handsome house on the Esplanade in New Orleans, for which they were to pay $16,000, and bound themselves to pay $100,000 for Magnolia Mound, a sugar plantation near Baton Rouge. With the acreage went 32 slaves, stock, equipment and a house built before 1800 that stood on a high knoll overlooking the river.[18]

The social life, though, was so charming, and the hunting so good, that Archille neglected both his law practice and the sugar crops, and Magnolia Mound was lost in November of 1837.[19] The law practice collapsed soon after that, and back they came to Lipona—broke again.

Things went from bad to worse after that. Lipona and its 1,060 acres, 108 slaves, equipment, cattle, provisions and other effects were deeded to James Gadsden for payment of two notes at the Union Bank in the Spring of 1839.[20]

Catherine and Achille moved to Econchattie, a smaller plantation, and when Achille died in 1847, Catherine was left with a mountain of debts and her memories of a kaleidoscopic life that may not always have been happy, but certainly not ever dull.[21]

Just two years after Achille's death, the Bonapartes came back into power in France.

Ellen Call Long, in a biographical sketch written at the time of Catherine Murat's death in 1867, says, "Only two years after the death of Col. Murat, the Bonapartes were restored to their former prestige. ... The day for which Achille had so long watched came too late for him, but on the assembling of the family at Paris, Kate was there and received with appropriate

Catherine Murat at middle age.

Portrait by Claribel B. Jett

honor by the Emperor, who recognized her as a "Princess of France," bestowing upon her at the same time 125,000 francs with the privilege of using the royal livery, which she ever afterward did, even in her country home."[2][2]

Mrs. Long embellished history a bit, perhaps, in her eulogy. There's a letter from Catherine to her youngest brother, Achille Murat Willis, preserved in the DAR Museum in Washington, which puts a slightly different light on the circumstances of that visit to Paris. The letter is dated March 16, 1849, and is a discouraged report of Catherine's efforts to repay the Prince's debts. She hoped to meet some of them with her crops, but has had no word from the Gray estate, and fears "all hope from that quarter is dead."[2][3] A postscript says, "I have at present some idea of going to Europe if they will lend me the money. The President has given me a polite invitation as well as other prominent members of the family."[2][4]

The President was Louis Napoleon, who soon declared himself Napoleon III, Emperor of France. He was Achille Murat's first cousin, and one with whom Achille and Catherine had spent six pleasant months in England during the 1830s, while the Bonaparte nephews were trying to think of a way to regain lost family fortunes.

An article from a nineteenth century magazine called *Household* gives what seems like a better explanation of Catherine's money from Louis Napoleon than Mrs. Long's account, in view of the letter in the DAR files.

The article says, in part, "When Napoleon III ascended the throne, he invited his cousin's widow to Paris; sent her $40,000 to enable her to visit France, with the wardrobe and retinue suitable to her rank. Her reception by the Emperor and his household was most cordial.

"The title of Princess Murat was formally conferred, and every kind attention to contribute to her pleasure was shown."[2][5]

The article also says that the Emperor showed his continued regard for her some years later by allowing her an annuity of $5,000 as long as she lived.

President Louis Napoleon of the Second Republic became Napoleon III of the Second Empire in 1852, and that was the year Catherine bought her first Tallahassee property. One would suppose that a wardrobe and servants suitable to a Princess of France were not as costly then as they might be now, and that

Catherine came back to Florida with some of the $40,000 in her pocket.

In 1854, she paid $6,000 for 500 acres of land and the house which in 1966 was moved from Jackson Bluff road to the Tallahassee Junior Museum and restored.[26]

A deed on file at the Leon County courthouse indicates the house was built between 1838 and 1841. Catherine used it as a town house, spending part of her time here, and part at Econchattie Plantation.

At the beginning of the War Between the States, it was Catherine who fired the cannon to announce the secession of Florida from the Union, and she spent the years of the war doing all manner of work for the confederacy.

She was the first Vice-Regent for Florida of the Mount Vernon Ladies Association, and managed to raise $3,000 for the restoration of her great grand uncle's home—a nice amount—either then, or now.[27]

Catherine was not as fortunate in the management of her own finances.

A small item in the back of the Mount Vernon Ladies Association records for February, 1860, has this notation: "A Tallahassee (Florida) paper says that by a series of calamities the private fortunes of Mrs. Murat, the widow of the late Achille Murat, has become much embarrassed. . . . Her crop for the present year, as for the past, has proved a failure—this year nearly destroyed by unfavorable seasons. During the past year we regret to record the loss by fire of a roadside Inn, established by the late Col. Achille Murat, for the accommodation of the public, which by the generosity of Mrs. Murat was tenanted by a colony of poor German emigrants. Add to this the loss of all the mules of her plantation by the crushing of a barn during a severe gale, and the subsequent loss of crops, and pecuniary embarrassment will readily be accounted for."[28]

Early in 1867, Catherine was stricken with typhoid fever, and after a six months illness died, in August, at Econchattie Plantation.

She is buried beside her Prince in the old Episcopal cemetery on Call Street, their graves marked with tall marble shafts.

NOTES

1. Adelaide Rutherford Willis, *The Willis Family of Virginia and Some of Their Descendants* (Mobile, Alabama: Paper work, 1967), p. 79 (hereafter cited as Willis, *Willis Family*).

Bonapartes at Murat graves
Prince and Princess Charles Murat during visit to Tallahassee's Episcopal
Cemetery in 1932.

2. Louise Pecquet du Bellet, *Some Prominent Virginia Families*, 4 vols. (Lynchburg, Virginia: J. P. Bell, 1907), 2: 290. For a family chart see Willis, *Willis Family*, illustration facing p. 5.

3. A. J. Hanna, *A Prince in Their Midst: The Adventurous Life of Achille Murat on the American Frontier* (Norman: University of Oklahoma Press, 1946), p. 116 (hereafter cited as Hanna, *Prince*).

4. Willis, *Willis Family*, p. 32.

5. Hanna, *Prince*, p. 118.

6. Ibid., pp. 68, 72, 73, 80, 103, 104.

7. Ibid., 110.

8. The Mission was on a hill just north of Mission Road and west of Ocala Road in modern Tallahassee.

9. Hanna, *Prince*, p. 119.

10. Ibid., p. 122.

11. Ellen Call Long, *Florida Breezes; or Florida, New and Old* (Gainesville: University of Florida Press, 1962), p. 154 (hereafter cited as Long, *Florida Breezes*).

12. Ibid.

13. O. T. Hammond to Harvey Hubbard, November, 1938, Florida State Library.

14. Long, *Florida Breezes*, p. 158.

15. Ibid., p. 157.

16. Ibid., pp. 158-159.

17. Harley L. Freeman, *Florida Obsolete Notes and Scrip* (Glen Ridge, New Jersey: Society of Paper Money Collectors, 1967), p. 90.

18. Hanna, *Prince*, p. 210.

19. Ibid., p. 211.

20. Ibid., p. 216.

21. Ibid., pp. 223, 231.

22. Ellen Call Long, "Princesse Achille Murat: A Biographical Sketch," *The Florida Historical Society Quarterly* (July 1909) 2: 33 (hereafter cited as Long, "Princesse Murat").

23. Willis, *Willis Family*, p. 117.

24. Ibid., p. 118.

25. "The Princess Murat: Nee Catherine Dangerfield Willis," *The Household*, p. 6, Xerox copy, undated, Florida State Library.

26. Deed Book K, January 9, 1854, p. 586, Leon County Courthouse.

27. Long, "Princesse Murat", p. 35.

28. Elswyth Thane Beebe, *Mount Vernon is Ours: The Story of its Preservation* (New York: Duell, Sloan and Pearce, 1966), pp. 96-97.

Chapter Seven

Designed in Detroit

Judge Augustus Brevoort Woodward left a clear mark on the history of Michigan; but his grave in Tallahassee is lost.

He was a friend and disciple of Thomas Jefferson with the same broad range of interests and inclinations toward innovation in government, science and education.

As a pioneer in city planning he laid out the city of Detroit; its main street still bears his name. He created, named and sold the city of Ypsilanti.

As Jefferson was setting up the University of Virginia, Woodward was drawing the original plan of education for the University of Michigan.

He had been a dominant figure in the frontier government of Michigan territory for almost 19 years, but accepted appointment to Middle Florida's first federal judgeship as something of a consolation prize after a campaign of falsehoods by his enemies succeeded in ousting him as Chief Justice of Michigan.

The eccentric bachelor jurist fit well into the rustic society of frontier Florida, especially with the equally unpredictable and innovative Prince Achille Murat, who became his close friend.

Judge Woodward didn't live long enough to found a new career in Florida; and he already was making powerful opponents with his judicial decisions against the government when he died on June 12, 1827, in his 52nd year.[1]

Woodward was born in New York City in 1774, into a family of old Dutch American lineage.[2]

A year later his father, John Woodward, an importer and merchant, raised a company of artillery and became its captain. When the British army took over New York City Captain

58

Judge Augustus B. Woodward
Drawing from Description

Detroit Free Press

Detroit Planner
Florida Judge

Woodward led his company away into the Continental army and stayed away seven years until the British occupation was ended. He was one of 13 patriots chosen to design a special badge for New Yorkers who had been exiled during the American war for independence.[3]

Augustus Woodward, who seems to have been christened "Elias" but changed his given name, enrolled in Columbia College at the age of 15 and promptly asserted an individuality that became a hallmark of his character, at times a source of derision which he may even have exploited as a quirk of personality.

"An insatiable thirst of admiration is a silly weakness," he wrote in a notebook. "Of what value is the enthusiastic admiration of another? A steady approbation of one's associates may prove highly serviceable to us, but mere admiration is of no value and is frequently the forerunner of contempt and esteem. . . ."[4]

As with so many of Woodward's ideas and propositions which seemed to be far ahead of his time, we are tempted to speculate that he saw himself as a sort of Cyrano de Bergerac, the tragi-comic figure created by the French novelist Rostand 70 years after the judge had died. The similarity of Cyrano and Woodward is striking—both tall, ungainly, bearing enormous noses and bold imaginations. Woodward asked a friend to do his unsuccessful wooing, even as Rostand's Cyrano did in an attempt to win his Roxane.[5]

Out of college, Woodward moved to Georgetown, Virginia, and was practicing law there when Washington, D.C., was established as the national Capital. He owned property in the new federal district and was on its first appointed governing board, though he advocated from the very beginning that it should have the home rule which still is denied it. He was in the first group of 11 lawyers admitted to practice in the new Capital; and to him is recorded the questionable distinction of losing the District of Columbia's first capital case. He won a short reprieve from his mentor, President Jefferson, but his client was hanged.

Woodward was acquainted with the French planner Pierre Charles L'Enfant, who laid out the streets of Washington. So when he arrived in Detroit in 1805 to find a frontier village burned to the ground less than a month earlier, it was natural that he should accept the challenge of creating a city on a new plan above the ashes.

Nor was this alien to his role as newly appointed chief justice of the Michigan territory. The law of the territory put all government in the hands of a legislative board composed of the governor, secretary and the three judges of the supreme court. Together, they made the law, enforced it, and administered the affairs of the territory.

Judge Woodward's first task at Detroit, then, was more ministerial than judicial. He drew out a long range plan for development of a city with streets running in equilateral triangles with broad plazas every 4,000 feet. The plan was abandonned after a dozen years, mostly because frontiersmen didn't take to the idea of being told where to build and live. But a trace of the plan still exists, and the main street of Detroit is Woodward avenue. Judge Woodward meant the main street to be Jefferson avenue; but the vagaries of development took the traffic down the thoroughfare to which he had attached his own name. It's about the only thing in Detroit that identifies him. (Tallahassee has a Woodward avenue, too, bisecting the Florida State University campus, but it is derived from another family, no kin, which came on the scene decades after he passed.)[6]

The Woodward plan was far ahead of its time. A century later, the modern urban planner, Frederick Law Olmstead, Jr., said "nearly all the most serious mistakes of Detroit's past have arisen from disregard of the spirit of Woodward's plan."[7]

The judge apparently took no part in planning the new capital city of Florida. The general outline had been drawn before him; and on January 7, 1825, a few days after he arrived in Tallahassee to take his place on the bench he wrote to the Secretary of State John Quincy Adams:

> Sir, I had the honor of mentioning to you, at Washington, that, after my arrival here, I should, probably, forward to you a report on the state of the country.
>
> I found that the public measures here had been modelled, according to my conception, with such sound judgment, and with such resolution and foresight, as to render unnecessary a farther prosecution of that intention.[8]

Woodward, as a jurist, tickled and irritated the backwoods French and American population of Michigan. Justice was informal. The courtroom was wherever the case dictated. Sometimes when testimony before the three judges became boring the chief justice would ask the clerk to mark him absent, then tip back his chair against the wall and take a nap.

Since the three Michigan judges held the majority on the governing board, they were said at times to handle an inadequacy of law in a case by adjourning as a court, turning themselves into a legislature and closing or opening the loophole as the situation demanded.

Nevertheless, Judge Woodward seems to have been both capable and deliberate when it came to moulding the major law of the territory within limitations allowed by the Northwest Ordinance which supplied an inexact basis for goverance of the territory.

Half a century before the issue of slavery split the nation, Judge Woodward declared his opposition. In a case involving the Denison family, which was claimed in slavery by a Detroiter, the judge said "the slave trade is unquestionably the greatest of enormities which have been perpetrated by the human race. The existence at this day of an absolute and unqualified slavery of the human species in the United States is universally and justly considered their greatest and deepest reproach."[9] Notwithstanding his feelings, he ruled possession of slaves in the territory was not unlawful and the Denisons must be considered the property of their owners. A few weeks later, slaves of British citizens escaped to Michigan, and Woodward ruled there was no treaty to require their return to Canada. The Denisons thereupon quietly slipped across the river to freedom on his precedent that if slaves couldn't be returned to Canada, they couldn't be brought back from Canada.

While he was occupied with the day to day business of politics and jurisprudence in trying to bring American law to the French, English and Indian population of Michigan, Woodward did not set aside his scholarly pursuits.

He undertook from boyhood to establish a system of classification and nomenclature for the whole realm of human science. He published his work in 1816 as "A System of Universal Science" or—to use the Greek language on which he based his names—"ecanthol epistemia."

Jefferson, who had talked with Woodward of such a system to catalog his library, called the judge's work "a monument to learning of the author and of the analyzing powers of his mind."[10]

The Woodward epistemia didn't catch on, perhaps because so few in a new country not yet attuned to scientific research understood it or took the bother to try.

A year after it was published, Judge Woodward and a few other Michigan officials set out to bring higher education and culture to the frontier.

Woodward wrote an act, and the legislative board adopted it, to create a system of education far ahead of anything then known in the nation. He called it "an act to establish the catholepistemiad, or University of Michigandia."[1] [1]

The university was to have 13 "didaxiisms" corresponding to the colleges or departments of large modern universities, each emphasizing a major branch of learning—and each bearing its Greek name according to the Woodward epistemia. Woodward even anticipated co-education, with "instructrixes."

The "Catholepistemiad" was set up. Woodward presided at ceremonies laying the cornerstone for his institution and selected two capable friends for its president and vice president.[1] [2]

But, like his classification of knowledge, it was all Greek to the untutored Michiganders. The institution lived, but on a more modest level, and the Woodward plan with its unpronounceable names was scrapped, though its counterpart today has academic similarities.

More enduring has been the Greek name "Ypsilanti" given by the judge to the Michigan town he developed on land he owned, and sold off to residents and business men. He chose Ypsilanti out of admiration for two brothers who were famous in his day for their fight to bring independence to Greece.

Woodward also wrote a pamphlet, very sophisticated for his time, on the composition of the sun and the "electrons" to which he ascribed the source of its light and energy.

He wrote another paper proposing that the U.S. presidency be a council of five men, serving in order of precedence according to the number of votes each received in the election. They would serve five-year terms, one dropping off the board annually to be replaced by a new man. The five would be selected regionally—almost exactly as many modern cities and counties are administered.

It would take three votes to constitute an act of the presidency. "He who acts alone is often exposed to error; and is not seldom liable to caprice," Woodward explained. "In the administration of public affairs the will of a simple individual ought not, perhaps, prevail even where there is right."

And there would be "government in the sunshine" as we have come to call it:

"A certain degree of publicity must attend the transactions of every political body," the judge said. "There is no stronger fortification to the frail virtue of man than the certainty his conduct is truly before the world."[1][3]

He sent the first copy of his "Considerations on the Executive" to Jefferson, who asked for several more.

Woodward campaigned successfully for the right of Michigan people to select their own officials, instead of appointed ones like himself. When Congress finally bestowed home rule on the territory, he ran three times for delegate to Congress, but was defeated each time.

Probably no man could have served in the dual capacity of chief justice and governing board member of that turbulent Michigan frontier without making enemies. Woodward had his share. The governor under whom he served first, with considerable disagreement, once was condemned to die for his actions in the war of 1812. Woodward was unjustly charged with conniving with the British who occupied Detroit during that conflict. Twice, his impeachment as a judge was suggested to Congress, but was not seriously considered.

He came through this all fairly clean, and his name was on President Monroe's list for reappointment as chief justice of Michigan territory under the new home-rule government in 1824. At the last minute before his name was sent for the Senate, the President scratched it off and substituted the name of John Hunt.

Hunt personally had brought to Washington statements and affidavits accusing Judge Woodward of coming to court intoxicated. When Woodward heard of the charges, he hurried to Washington with affidavits to explain he really had made an extra effort to get to court at all that day because he was so ill his doctor had dosed him up with medicine and brandy to help him leave his sick bed. The medication had made him appear intoxicated.

President Monroe accepted Woodward's explanation; but it was too late to save his position on the Michigan supreme court. Instead, he was offered the judgeship for the new middle district of Florida, which would give the Tallahassee area the same judicial set-up as East and West Florida had from the beginning of territorial Florida four years earlier.

Judge Woodward went back to Detroit, put all his property up for sale, was given a farewell party in which even some of his more vitriolic opponents joined—then took off for the new Florida territory at the bottom of the nation.[14]

He found at Tallahassee a far better form of government, with more amenable judicial duties than he had encountered on the Michigan frontier nearly 20 years before, though the village capital was hardly more developed than the burned-out Detroit when he first saw it.

Whereas in Detroit he had been both law-maker and judge, in Tallahassee he was only a judge.

The legislative power of the Florida territory was "vested in the governor, and in thirteen of the most fit and discreet persons of the territory, to be called the Legislative Council, who shall be appointed annually by the President of the United States, by and with consent of the Senate from among the citizens of the United States residing in Florida."[15]

Woodward found this machinery in full operation when he arrived in Tallahassee under his commission as U.S. District Judge. On an earlier trip to look over the territory in 1824 before returning to Michigan to settle affairs, the Legislative Council had pressed him into service unofficially to settle a dispute over public and private ownership of land in the capital. Back in Florida, officially seated, one of Judge Woodward's first acts was to set up the territory's first court of appeals. He and the judges from the other two districts were to meet once a year to hear appeals from lower court decisions. The appellate court's decisions, in turn, could be taken to the Supreme Court of the United States.

On January 3, 1825, Judge Woodward wrote tersely from Tallahassee to Secretary of State John Quincy Adams:

The Court of Appeals of the Territory of Florida was this day, fully organized, according to law, and it has been conceived proper to apprize the Department of State of the circumstance.[16]

It was the effective beginning of Florida's first formal judicial system.

Judge Woodward's duties in Tallahassee do not seem to have been onerous nor very complicated.

He found congenial companions in Tallahassee. He attended Florida's first Masonic lodge, but never transferred his membership to it. He founded the Florida Institute of Agricultural Antiquities and Science. (Later to be known simply as the

Florida Agricultural Society.) Woodward was its first president. James Gadsden was first vice president, Governor Duval second vice president, Prince Achille Murat third vice president, and Byrd C. Willis (Murat's father-in-law) fourth vice president—an influential hierarchy, indeed.[17]

However his capacity for ingenious projects seemed to have been drained by the time he reached Florida. It's a pity, for example, that he didn't take an interest in digging a canal across Florida, which was proposed early in the territorial period and has been a recurrent project ever since. Remembering that he once planned a project much like the modern St. Lawrence seaway linking the Atlantic with the Great Lakes, it would be interesting to have on record a design from Woodward's fertile mind for a Florida cross state canal.

Perhaps his most important court rulings involved land claims under the pre-emption act which gave settlers on Florida public lands prior to January 1, 1825, the right to purchase them at a limited price in preference to others.

Numerous lawsuits were filed under the pre-emption act on land taken over for the town of Tallahassee after the first settlers arrived; but the most difficult case arose when Governor Duval claimed pre-emption rights to a homesite he had selected on land which Congress gave to General Lafayette.[18]

Woodward ruled in Duval's favor, but the Governor agreed to take up land in the township southeast of the Capitol in order to let Lafayette have the whole township to the northeast. The case was dragged on through the courts for several years after Woodward's death on Duval's claim for reimbursement of outlays he made for a home and beginning of a plantation on the land which went to Lafayette.

Richard Keith Call and George W. Ward, in charge of the Tallahassee land sales, harshly criticized Judge Woodward for his ruling that pre-emptive rights could be claimed for as little as one-eighth of a section of land contrary to their interpretation and instructions from Washington that the least pre-emption could be claimed for a quarter section. They also questioned his rulings on validity of some claims.[19]

Two weeks after Judge Woodward died they wrote to George Graham, U.S. Land Commissioner, that in some of the cases "it is a fact well known that Judge Woodward never examined the evidence . . . and that his clerk was directed to issue his writs to the applicants on abstract questions."[20] They said they were

submitting evidence "of the inattention and incapability of
Judge Woodward at that period to discharge his official duties."[2] [1]

The judge apparently had been sick of some illness that is
not recorded, for nothing from him appears in official papers
for two months before his death on June 12, 1827.

He was given a Masonic funeral, probably from the home of
George Fisher, whose tavern had been the scene of a welcoming
dinner two years before. Minutes of a special June 13, 1825
session of Florida's oldest Masonic Lodge, Jackson No. 1 of
Tallahassee, report the brothers, including Call, accompanied
the body of A. B. Woodward to the place of interment, where
the usual rituals were conducted, "after which lodge was closed
with peace and harmony."

Thus passed a character who in life had experienced little real
peace and harmony. The lodge minutes do not record the place
of burial, and no Woodward marker has been found in
Tallahassee's earliest graveyards.

NOTES

1. Elizabeth Gaspar Brown, "Judge Augustus Brevoort Woodward: Man
of Property," *Michigan History*, (1956) 40: 198.

2. Unless otherwise noted the material for this chapter came from Frank
B. Woodford, *Mr. Jefferson's Disciple: A Life of Justice Woodward* (East
Lansing, Michigan: The Michigan State College Press, 1953) (hereafter
cited as Woodford, *Disciple*).

3. *Detroit Free Press*, February 28, 1909.

4. Woodford, *Disciple*, p. 19.

5. Woodward was even more ambitious than Cyrano. He instructed his
friend McCloskey to engage in a proxy courtship with two belles of
Detroit—simultaneously! One, Monique Navarre, claimed descent from the
Bourbon kings of France.

6. Woodward Street in Tallahassee was named for William T. Woodward,
who in the early 1900s owned land immediately south of the present
Florida State University campus.

7. Woodford, *Disciple*, p. 41.

8. Clarence E. Carter, ed., *The Territorial Papers of the United States*, 27
vols. (Washington, D.C.: United States Government Printing Office, 1958),
23: 153 (hereafter cited as Carter, *Territorial Papers*).

9. Woodford, *Disciple*, p. 86.

10. Ibid., p. 153.

11. Ibid., p. 157.

12. Rev. John Montieth, a graduate of Princeton who conducted
non-denominational services in Detroit, was named president. Father
Gabriel Richard, the local Roman Catholic priest, was chosen as vice
president.

13. Woodford, *Disciple*, p. 133.

14. The tribute read in part, "that the extensive legal information, incorruptible integrity, splendid talents, correct and gentlemanly deportment, tried partiotism and great literary acquirements of the Hon. Augustus B. Woodward, eminently entitle him to the respect of every American." Ibid., p. 179.

15. Carter, *Territorial Papers*, 22: 391.

16. Ibid., 23: 151.

17. Mary Lamar Davis, "Tallahassee Through Territorial Days," *Apalachee* (1944): 47-61.

18. Duval claimed that he "settled on and improved" the quarter section in the summer of 1824, prior to its being granted to General Lafayette in 1825. Carter, *Territorial Papers*, 23: 993.

19. Ibid., 23: 725-726.

20. Ibid., 23: 875-876.

21. Ibid., 23: 875.

Chapter Eight

Gadsden – Name on the Map

James Gadsden, alone among all the progeny of American founding patriots who pioneered in Florida, stands higher in the history books than his Revolutionary ancestor.

He was a key figure in territorial Florida—Indian fighter and Indian treaty negotiator. He went on to become minister to Mexico and arrange the acquisition of Arizona and New Mexico, which still appear on some maps as "The Gadsden Purchase."

For that effort, he overshadows his grandfather, Gen. Christopher Gadsden, a radical South Carolina leader who distinguished himself as a revolutionary, calling for a colonial union against recognition of the British parliament in the Stamp Act Congress 11 years before the Declaration of Independence. Christopher Gadsden was one of South Carolina's four delegates to the Continental Congress in 1774. Six months before the Declaration of Independence was signed, he left Congress and already was in the field as a senior colonel in the South Carolina revolutionary force. In June of 1776, while Congress was drafting the Declaration, Christopher Gadsden was in command of Fort Johnson when the British attacked Charleston at Fort Moultrie, opposite his position, and were repulsed.

General Gadsden roiled the conservative revolutionaries of South Carolina, though, by working successfully for disestablishment of the church and popular election of Senators in the South Carolina constitution. Opponents, led by John Rutledge, nullified his leadership by electing him vice president of the assembly. Later, in a ruckus with the Governor over command

James Gadsden
Portrait by Claribel B. Jett — Copied from miniature painted 1821-22,
owned by Mrs. James R. Kitter.

of the continental troops, he resigned his command and fought
a bloodless duel with Gen. Robert Howe of North Carolina. He
sat out part of the war as a parolee of the British in close
confinement at St. Augustine; but returned to sit in the South
Carolina convention which ratified the United States Constitution in 1789. Later, he was a member of the convention that
drafted the constitution of the state of South Carolina.[1]

But who ever heard of Christopher Gadsden? It's James
Gadsden, the grandson, we read about—and for whom a county
in Florida, a street in Tallahassee, a city in Alabama and another
in Arizona are named.

James Gadsden, at the age of 30, was playing a spectacular
role in the Apalachee area six years before Tallahassee was
selected as the seat of Florida government. He had an
Apalachicola river fort named for him before Florida even was
acquired from Spain by the United States. He helped establish
the territorial government, was a planter in virgin soil, an early
bank organizer, Indian treaty negotiator—but a failure in
electoral politics—before he moved on to railroad development
in the Carolinas and his arrangement of western land purchase
from Mexico.

Gadsden, the grandson, was born in Charleston in 1788. He
was educated at Yale, and entered business in his hometown
after graduation in 1806. But he soon turned to a military
career under the command and sponsorship of Gen. Andrew
Jackson through the War of 1812 and Jackson's campaign
against the Indians of Spanish Florida in 1818.[2]

It was Lt. James Gadsden who seized the correspondence
Jackson used to convict and execute the British traders,
Ambrister and Arbuthnot, after a drumhead court martial at
Spanish St. Marks.

It was Gadsden, also, who erected an American fort at
Prospect Bluff in Spanish territory on the Apalachicola River
which remained in American hands until the United States
acquired Florida several years later. The Fort was named for
him, and now is the site of a state park.[3]

By the time Jackson was named to take over Florida as
military governor, Gadsden had become a colonel. He was
appointed adjutant general, but the U.S. Senate refused to
confirm him. He resigned from the army, as many others did,
rather than accept a reduced rank in the total reduction of
armed forces after the War of 1812.[4] Gadsden became a sort of

advance man for Jackson in his takeover of Florida government.

Old Hickory appointed him his "confidential agent." He sent him from Pensacola to St. Augustine with orders for the transfer of East Florida from Spanish to American control. He assigned Gadsden to receive the transfer at St. Marks, the only other Spanish holding—besides Pensacola and St. Augustine— where the change of flags was done ceremonially.[5]

Gadsden put his bets on the new Florida frontier.

He was appointed by President Monroe to survey the line behind which the Seminole Indians would be forced to withdraw.[6]

Jackson had proposed that they be held to a reservation along the Apalachicola river, a few miles from the Gulf coast and with their backs to Georgia and Alabama, whereby they could be kept under control. But that was before the Apalachicola area—Apalachee, Middle Florida—was opened to white settlers and Tallahassee was established at its center as territorial capital.

The government plan was to push the Seminoles into extreme southwest Florida, in the Big Cypress swamp region. However, Gadsden was instructed by Secretary of War John C. Calhoun if "you should find that the northern line, as defined in the treaty, does not embrace a sufficiency of good land for the accommodation of the Indians, you are authorized to exercise a sound discretion and remove it farther north so as to include the necessary quantity."[7]

Though Gadsden personally preferred to move the Seminoles out of Florida entirely he agreed that South Florida—now so rich and populous—was no fit place for Indians to have to live.[8] He acknowledged their complaint that not even hickory nuts could be gathered in the Big Cypress. He moved the northern line from their preserve to the vicinity of modern Ocala, and proposed for them a large elliptical reservation encompassing most of the fruitful lake and ridge section of Florida. He reported to Calhoun on June 15, 1824:

> "Restore confidence—ensure protection—and steadily persevere in the annual distributions of stock of cattle and hogs contemplated, and within a few years the Florida Indians will be among the number of the best conditioned of the aborigines of America."[9]

Books still are being written about the dealing and dickering that followed. Omitting the tedious details, in essence Washing-

ton and white men balked. Send them south or move them
west. The Indians balked.

Gadsden and Bernard Segni, a native Floridian of Minorcan
extraction, were appointed to treaty with the Seminoles.
Governor Duval, back from one of his prolonged absences,
joined them. There was a big pow wow at Moultrie Creek, north
of St. Augustine, Gadsden made tough talk: Either the Indians
would accede to the white man's terms, or the white man's
army would move against them.

The Indians agreed to take land on the north side of
Charlotte Harbor instead of the swampier area to the south. Six
chiefs, mostly from Apalachee, agreed to smaller areas from two
to eight miles square in the Apalachicola valley.

It was clearly a coerced treaty and the Seminoles showed no
hurry to comply; but the white settlers hoped it would give
them lands to spread out in with peace.[10]

Mission accomplished, Gadsden turned his eyes to the life of
a planter in the rich land just opening up around the new capital
at Tallahassee.

On his various surveying and political trips to St. Augustine,
he had met Prince Achille Murat, who had bought a plantation
south of St. Augustine but was always ready to swing out on a
new venture. The two bachelors formed a partnership. Murat
sold out in East Florida, borrowed some money from Gadsden's
brother in Charleston, and together they bought raw land 15
miles east of Tallahassee in Jefferson County. They named their
plantation Wacissa and set about clearing it themselves, stripped
to the waist and sweating in the sun like common labor. Though
they enjoyed the carefree back to nature approach to taming
the wilderness, neither partner was cut out for the steady labor
of clearing, planting and hoping to harvest.[11]

Gadsden bought out Murat by taking up his notes. Murat
borrowed elsewhere and bought the neighboring plantation,
Lipona, where he took his bride from Tallahassee to their log
cabin complex of dwellings.

Gadsden, a merchant soon turned soldier in his early
manhood, now tried other pursuits along with his planting. He
had been appointed to Florida's first territorial legislative
council in 1822, but before the council met he resigned to be
Jackson's confidential agent.[12] With the Indians temporarily
off the warpath, he moved around the territory—exploring,
surveying, politicking.

He became officer in charge of inland waterways and road supervision. He started the inland waterway linking the St. Marys and St. Johns rivers, and improved harbors there and at St. Marks. He helped draw the route for the road from St. Augustine to Pensacola, prime project of the territory. He was commissioned, also, to route a road from Cape Florida below modern Miami up the east coast to St. Augustine. Gadsden gave up on that. He reported to the quartermaster general that a waterway would be more practical.

"The population from the real poverty of the country south of the Moschetto (now Indian River) never can be dense," he said, "and consequently will not be capable of preserving the road from dilapidation after completed."[13] He should hear the clamor for more interstate highways to serve the millions along that Gold Coast of Florida today!

In 1825, Gadsden ran for delegate to Congress but was beaten by his Jefferson County neighbor Joseph M. White. He ran again in 1827, 1829 and 1831, but lost each time. At one point the 1831 election was declared a tie by Governor Duval, but the special election he called to settle it never was held. White continued in office.[14] Gadsden's old sponsor, Andrew Jackson, was President by this time. He might have helped Gadsden, but their relationship had cooled over Gadsden's reported espousal of the doctrine that a state could use its sovereign power to nullify an act of the federal government.[15]

By 1832, the Indians had become so troublous again that the War Department issued orders for a special agent to negotiate another treaty with the Seminoles. The job went to Gadsden, whose treaty of Moultrie Creek nine years earlier didn't take. That time his orders were to persuade them to move west.

They parleyed at Payne's Landing on the Oklawaha River. A treaty was signed there, but the terms and understanding have forever been in dispute. Some chiefs later repudiated their signatures. Each side accused the other of bad faith. Authority was disputed. A crucial point was the white man's assignment of the Florida Indians to the Creek nation in the west. This was abomination to the Seminoles, for the Creeks had been their traditional enemies. Moreover, many runaway slaves had joined the Seminoles, and the Creeks had historically conspired with Southern whites for return of slaves. Some historians say it was the blacks among the Seminoles who led the rebellion against the movement to lands in the West.[16]

Anyway, the Seminole War was on in earnest. It would last 10 years and call forth the whole military power of the United States under such heroes as Gen. Zachary Taylor, later president, and Gen. Winfield Scott, who ran against him and lost. The little remnant of Seminole tribes never was conquered by troops who never learned to counter their guerrilla tactics of striking, then fading into the glades and woods of sub-tropical Florida.

Gadsden caught some of the blame for it, though most white people probably backed him in his effort to move all the Seminoles to Oklahoma. Before it was over, he wound up his affairs in Florida and moved back to South Carolina in 1839.

A year later, Gadsden was president of the Louisville, Cincinnati and Charleston railroad, which was struggling to extend its tracks westward in the face of national financial distress. He had ambition to tie together a network of small lines all the way through the South to the Pacific coast, with Charleston to serve it as an Atlantic terminal for shipping to Europe. His plan was thus to break the South's dependence on the Northeast for vital industrial supplies. He organized and attended numerous conventions throughout the South in an effort to bring it about. In 1850, though, stockholders of his little railroad became impatient over lack of dividends and replaced him as president.

He was appointed Minister to Mexico by President Franklin Pierce on the recommendation of Jefferson Davis, who was Secretary of War. One of his missions was to obtain enough land for a railroad right of way through Mexican territory to California. This was part of his own planned route to the Pacific. With authority to buy as much land as he could for $50 million from the financially pressed Mexican dictator Santa Anna, Gadsden cast his eyes on much of the northern part of the nation below the Rio Grande, including all lower California.

He had to settle for what now is New Mexico and Arizona. The railroad went through them to California.[17] James Gadsden didn't live to see it, but he wrote his dream and his name of the map of American expansion—from the frontier of Florida to the far edge of the western frontier.

NOTES

1. This short sketch of Christopher Gadsden was compiled from Allen Johnson and Dumas Malone (eds), *Dictionary of American Biography* (New York: Charles Scribners' Sons, 1931), 7:82-83 (hereafter cited as Johnson and Malone, *American Biography*).

2. Ibid., p. 83.

3. Mark F. Boyd, "Events at Prospect Bluff on the Apalachicola River, 1808-1818," *The Florida Historical Quarterly* 16 (October, 1937):90.

4. John K. Mahon, *History of the Second Seminole War 1835-1842* (Gainesville: University of Florida Press, 1967), p. 40 (hereafter cited as Mahon, *Seminole War*).

5. Clarence E. Carter, ed., *The Territorial Papers of the United States*, 27 vols. (Washington, D.C.: United States Government Printing Office, 1956), 22: 140 (hereafter cited as Carter, *Territorial Papers*).

6. Ibid., p. 783.

7. Ibid.

8. Mahon, *Seminole War*, p. 41.

9. Carter, *Territorial Papers*, 22:969.

10. Mahon, *Seminole War*, pp. 41-49.

11. A. J. Hanna, *A Prince in Their Midst: The Adventurous Life of Achille Murat on the American Frontier* (Norman: University of Oklahoma Press, 1946), pp. 104-105.

12. Carter, *Territorial Papers*, 22:913.

13. Ibid., 23:127.

14. Ibid., 24: 539.

15. Ellen Call Long, *Florida Breezes: or Florida New and Old* (Gainesville: University of Florida Press, 1962), pp. 81, 143. Johnson and Malone *American Biography*, 7:83.

16. Mahon, *Seminole War*, pp. 75-85.

17. The material for Gadsden's life after 1839 came from Johnson and Malone, *American Biography*, 7: 83-84.

Chapter Nine

The Henry Bloodline

Patrick Henry, who ignited the fires of American revolution, may have preferred the campfires of Virginia's hunting grounds.

His grandson, Dr. Thomas Y. Henry, who came to Florida and settled at Quincy about the year of statehood (1845) was of the same bent.[1] His legacy became a famous strain of foxhounds which still join the chase in southern fields. The Henry hounds, known nowadays as the Birdsong dogs, outlived Dr. Henry's considerable public service to Florida during the Confederacy.

Thomas Y. was one of several grandchildren of the red-haired patriot. He was born in 1821 at Red Hill, the plantation Patrick Henry purchased in 1795 near Appomattox, Va. The orator of those famous lines ". . . give me liberty, or give me death" died and was buried at Red Hill 22 years before Thomas Y. was born there. The grandson lived at Red Hill as a boy, was educated as a medical doctor and came to Florida as a tuberculosis patient in his mid-twenties.[2]

The Florida climate agreed with him, for he lived nearly 30 years before he died there. His grave in Quincy's Western cemetery is marked by a small stone which bears the terse inscription:

Dr. Thomas Y. Henry
Grandson of Patrick Henry.
Born at Red Hill, Va. 1821.
Died May 31, 1869.

He had been active as a practicing physician and druggist at Quincy. J. Randall Stanley, in his 1948 "History of Gadsden County" wrote that "for over two years" during the Civil War "scenes of great suffering were daily occurrences in the village's improvised hospitals. When Dr. T. Y. Henry was appointed by Governor (John) Milton in 1863 to establish hospital facilities in West Florida, he converted Quincy churches and public buildings into temporary facilities for the lack of better."[3]

Dr. Henry was deeply involved in the cause of the Confederacy, as his grandfather no doubt would have been if he had been alive (for Patrick Henry was so distrustful of the federal union that he led the state righters who opposed Virginia ratification of the United States Constitution).[4] The grandson, then, was following ancestral tradition when he went as a delegate from Gadsden county to the convention at Tallahassee which adopted the resolution of secession from the union in 1861. He sat with the convention for drafting the new constitution which governed the Confederate State of Florida from 1861 to 1865, when the Confederacy fell and Florida rejoined the union. He served in the State Legislature for three years (1862-64) during the Civil War.[5]

He was a leading Mason, had served as Worshipful Master of Quincy's Washington Lodge No. 2 (F. and A.M.) several times, and was grandmaster of Florida Masonry in 1857-58.[6]

He had long ago given away the famous pack of foxhounds he had brought from Virginia because Florida alligators were decimating the kennels; but before he died, he wrote (left-handed, because his right had been paralyzed by a stroke) bragging that "there are no foxhounds anywhere to be found that can speed or stay with these dogs."

"I am the originator of them," he wrote in 1867 to Col. Haiden C. Trigg of Glasgow, Kentucky, who later mixed the Henry hound strain with others to produce the Trigg dog still sworn by among some fox hunters.[7]

It seems likely that, if he had written his own tombstone inscription, Dr. Henry would have ranked his dog breeding accomplishments along with his ancestry; and Grandfather Patrick probably wouldn't have minded.

Thomas Jefferson who had sat with Henry in the Virginia House of Burgesses and was stirred by his oratorical onrushes against the British Crown, knew that Patrick loved the hunt.

Jefferson scoffed at passages in William Wirt's biography of Patrick Henry which reported the patriot read "Plutarch's Lives" once a year.

Patrick Henry
(1736-1799)
Revolutionary Leader
Governor of Virginia

Dictionary of American Portraits

Dr. Thomas Y. Henry
Florida secession
leader — breeder
of fine foxhounds

Enlarged from a group photograph of 1861 Secession convention in FSU Photo Archives.

"I don't believe he ever read two volumes of them," Mr. Jefferson was quoted in 1824.

On his visits to court, he used always to put up with me. On one occasion of the breaking up in November, to meet again in the spring, as he was departing in the morning, he looked among my books and observed, Mr. Jefferson I will take two volumes of Hume's Essays, and try to read them this winter. On his return, he brought them, saying he had not been able to get half way into them.

His great delight was to put on his hunting-shirt, collect a parcel of overseers and such-like people, and spend weeks together hunting in the 'piny woods,' camping at night and cracking jokes around a light-wood fire.

It was to him that we were indebted for the unanimity that prevailed among us. He would address the assemblages of the people at which he was present in such strains of native eloquence as Homer wrote in. I never heard any thing that deserved to be called by the same name with what flowed from him; and where he got that torrent of language from is inconceivable. I have frequently shut my eyes while he spoke, and, when he was done, asked myself what he had said, without being able to recollect a word of it. He was no logician. He was truly a great man, however—one of enlarged views.[8]

With such a heritage of love of the hunt in his blood, it is no wonder that young Dr. Thomas Y. Henry should turn early to fox hound breeding. The dog books give us more information about the Henry hound bloodline, since he started it, than we know about the doctor himself.

In Virginia Dr. Henry owned a pack of famous fox hounds he called "Irish hounds" because they were directly descended from "Mountain" and "Muse" which had been imported from Ireland. "The Modern Dog Encyclopedia" traces the strain:

Henry's dog "Captain" was given to him by Dr. James Buchanan, who got him from Capt. Charles Carroll, Jr., of Carrollton (both families prominent in American history). Captain was by Traveler out of Sophy, both by Mountain out of Muse.

From Captain, Dr. Henry wrote Colonel Trigg, he had first bred the strain in 1843 "from pure parent stock and a judicious system afterwards of selecting and crossing until I am of the opinion they are nearly perfection.

I hunted them in Virginia two years, against all comers and never found the first dog that could live with them in a red fox chase. The same thing can be said by Mr. Birdsong, to whom I gave the pack 21 years ago.[9]

George L. F. Birdsong, who lived at Thomaston, Ga., had sent by wagon to Virginia to get a pair of Captain's puppies from Dr. Henry.

The two dog fanciers became friends, and when Dr. Henry began his leisurely trip to Florida a few years later, Birdsong met the entourage and hunted along with Dr. Henry part of the trip.

At Quincy, Dr. Henry put his fox hounds in the field; but they couldn't resist the temptation to chase the abundant deer into swampy areas. Alligators caught so many of them that Dr. Henry feared for loss of the precious strain. He wrote and told Birdsong he could have them.

Birdsong wanted to call them the "Henry hounds," but his own name became attached to them because he was breeding them and showing them in competition.

Birdsong in 1861 crossed his Henry strain with a dog named "July." Though "July" was believed also to be a descendant of Dr. Henry's Captain, many fanciers thought the cross had strengthened the bloodlines. One branch of the Birdsong dogs thereby became known as "July hounds," the other remained the Birdsong strain which still is extant.

Later, Colonel Trigg obtained some puppies of both the Birdsong and July strains from Birdsong and bred them with Walker and Maupin hounds to get the Trigg strain of hounds which the Modern Dog Encyclopedia says "are generally equipped with splendid noses and are noted for exceptional speed and splendid endurance."[10]

Dr. Henry would be pleased at the report; so, too, would be his Grandfather Patrick.

Footnotes

1. *Tallahassee Democrat*, July 7, 1970.
2. J. Randall Stanley, *The History of Gadsden County* (Quincy, Florida: Gadsden County Times, 1948), unnumbered.
3. Ibid.
4. Patrick Henry was deeply involved in almost every aspect of revolutionary activity. He served on the first Virginia Committee of Correspondence and was a delegate to the Continental Congresses of 1774 and 1775. Henry also helped to draft the first state constitution of Virginia. Briefly commander of the Virginia armies, he resigned and was elected governor for three terms (1776-1778). From 1780 to 1790, Henry

was continuously in public service, either as a state legislator or governor. His opposition to the new federal constitution stemmed from his concern over navigation rights on the Mississippi as well as his fears for civil liberties and states' rights. Henry was largely responsible for the Bill of Rights and after its passage was reconciled to the Constitution.

5. "Whitfield's Notes," *Florida Statutes* (1941) 3: 159.

6. *Photographs and Statistics of Grand Marshals of Most Worshipful Grand Lodge F. and A.M.*, Issue No. 2 (1830-1973).

7. *Tallahassee Democrat*, July 7, 1970.

8. Sarah N. Randolph, *The Domestic Life of Thomas Jefferson* (Monticello-Charlottesville: Thomas Jefferson Memorial Foundation, 1947), p. 19. Jefferson not only supplied anecdotes, documents and memories of Henry to William Wirt, he also encouraged Wirt to press forward during the many difficulties of writing and publication of the biography.

9. *Tallahassee Democrat*, July 7, 1970.

10. Henry P. Davis, *The Modern Dog Encyclopedia* (Harrisburg, Pennsylvania: The Stackpole Co., 1953), p. 465.

Chapter Ten

California's Gain

Cosam Emir Bartlett's great uncle Josiah Bartlett signed the Declaration of Independence right under the big bold signature of John Hancock.

Half a century later, Cosam and his brother Myron were pushing a free and independent press through the Georgia and Florida frontiers. Cosam established Florida's first daily newspaper at Apalachicola. Three of his sons went west with their presses, and one became Governor of California.

Tracing the Bartletts of New England is as tedious and difficult as trying to sort out the Randolphs of Virginia.

Josiah, the Signer, was a son of Stephen and Mary (Webster) Bartlett of Massachusetts. He was a physician who began practice in Kingston, N.H., at the age of 21. Before he stepped deeply into the politics of the Revolutionary era, Dr. Bartlett was credited with a good many progressive medical reforms.

He was a member of the New Hampshire colonial legislature and was appointed by the royal governor as a colonel in the militia in 1767, but he was summarily dismissed in 1775 because he took the side of the colonies in the growing dispute with the mother country. By that time he already was a member of the Continental Congress, from which the committee was drawn to draft the Declaration of Independence. Because his name began with "B" it is said that it was second on the roll call for independence. However it happened, he signed second. He went back to New Hampshire to serve in order as chief justice of the Supreme Court (though he wasn't a lawyer), member of the convention for ratification of the U.S. Constitution, and governor.[1]

Cosam Emir Bartlett was a great grandson of Josiah's elder brother Stephen, with whom the Signer had settled a large grant of land in New Hampshire before the Revolution. There isn't much in the record about Stephen except that he sired a family which distinguished itself in pioneer southern and western journalism and politics.[2]

Cosam was trained as a lawyer and admitted to the bar of New Hampshire in 1815. Within a year, at the age of 22, he went south with his brother Myron and settled for a while on the staff of a Charleston paper—first as an editorial writer, then as editor. It was a transient occupation, and by February of 1817, Cosam was in Savannah as one of the publishers of the Columbian Museum. He apparently was associated with his brother Myron for a while in publishing the Macon Telegraph, but in 1828 he established the Savannah Mercury. In 1833, he was editor of The Democrat in Columbus. He may also have had a newspaper connection in Milledegville, when it was Georgia's capital.[3]

During his 19 years of newspapering in Georgia, the Territory of Florida was opening up, booming and beckoning Cosam Bartlett.

The Apalachicola Land Company had built a town at the mouth of the Apalachicola river as a rival development to old St. Joseph which was beginning to prosper a few miles to the west. It persuaded the veteran Georgia editor, then 42, to establish a new paper, the Apalachicola Gazette—Florida's first daily—in 1839. Bartlett already had been on the scene a couple of years and was active in the politics of Apalachicola. He was a member of the town council in 1837 and served part of a term as mayor. He was a member of the convention at St. Joseph which in the last days of 1838 and early 1839 drafted the constitution with which Florida entered statehood.[4]

His Gazette, like most papers in those days, was relatively short-lived though lively while it lasted. If Bartlett was beholden to the Apalachicola Land Company for any help in getting started, it apparently didn't show up in his editorial policies. One notable quarrel was over the company's property tax assessments. The company thought they were too high. The Gazette, whose publisher helped set them as a member of the town council, defended them as proper.

His reputation for journalistic independence and resolution is embellished by a family story later told by his grandson, Louis

Bartlett, about an incident in one of Cosam's Georgia newspaper shops.

> There is a tradition that my grandfather was a reformer and
> incurred the enmity of a group, who called upon him one day and
> told him they were going to string him up.
>   He was in his newspaper office at the time and, lighting a match,
> held it over a keg of gunpowder saying, 'Get out of here or we will
> all go to hell together'." They left.[5]

Whether it was disagreement with the land company or bad
times which had befallen Apalachicola after the national panic
of 1837, Bartlett moved to the capital in 1840, bought the
Tallahassee Star and renamed it the Star of Florida. He left the
Gazette in charge of his 16-year-old son, Washington Bartlett,
for a few months. The boy would learn his craft well and apply
his skills notably in California.[6]

Critics who have studied the press of territorial Florida rank
C. E. Bartlett among the best editors of his day, respected by
both those who opposed and those who supported his views as a
voice of the Whig party against the Democrats in the robust
politics of the period.

Joseph Clisby, editor of the Macon Telegraph, who earlier
had been editor of the Florida Sentinel in Tallahassee, wrote 18
years after the elder Bartlett's death that "The Tallahassee press
for a generation had been marked with unusual ability. At the
time we first knew it, Bartlett and Gibson, and 10 years after,
Dyke, were among the keenest of American writers, and to the
practical experience of a long life, added a vigour and acumen
unexcelled in the Country."[7]

Two of Cosam Bartlett's sons, Washington and Cosam Julian,
soon joined him in Tallahassee; and they became proprietors of
the Star in 1844. He continued to write for it occasionally in
the stirring days when Florida was leaving territorial status and
setting up a State government of the people's own election in
1845. The Bartletts continued in charge when the Star became
the Southern Journal in 1846, and until it was absorbed by the
pre-eminent Floridian.[8]

In 1848, gold was found in California. Washington took off
in the rush. Apparently he had no thought of panning for gold.
Washington surmised San Francisco would need a daily newspaper by the time he got there. He sent his printing equipment
over land, probably with a party of several men who left
Tallahassee together, and took a boat around the tip of South

America. His father moved back to Columbus, Georgia, where he died in 1850.

When Washington Bartlett arrived in San Francisco in November 1849, his equipment was awaiting him, and so was an illustrious career in western journalism and politics.

He divided his resources and started two papers instead of one—California's first daily, the Journal of Commerce in partnership with John S. Robb, and the Daily Alta California. Part of the strategy was to tap into the government printing which in those days was vital to the life of a newspaper.

He printed California's first book, "California As It Is and As It May Be: A Guide to the Gold Fields" before he had been there more than a few months.

His Daily Journal of Commerce jumped into the public affairs of the booming territory and became a staunch advocate of early California statehood.

In 1852, his brother Columbus Bartlett joined him in California and together they started the San Francisco Daily Evening News. A couple of years later, brother Julian came in to make it a family affair. Washington was in charge. Julian wrote the editorials. Columbus handled the business.

Washington soon was into active politics. In 1856 he was an organizer and participant of the Vigilance Committee, which wrote a constitution for citizen action outside the law to clean up the political corruption and crime that came with the gold rush and lingered in old San Francisco. The Evening News endorsed the committee along with Washington, though brothers Julian and Columbus refrained from active participation. Washington was captain of the military company which seized the jail and took custody of a couple of prisoners in a notorious action of the Vigilantes.

In 1856 he bought his brothers' interest in the Evening News and—with two partners—converted it into the morning daily called the "True Californian."[9]

It was, friends said, "brilliantly edited and extravagantly managed."[10] Publication was stopped in 1857, leaving Washington a debt it took him ten years to pay off.

Julian ended his days as an editorial writer for the San Francisco Bulletin. Washington moved further and further into politics—county clerk for three terms, four years in the State Senate, twice mayor of San Francisco in the 1880s.

He was elected Governor on the Democratic ticket in 1886

when nearly all other Democrats were defeated, and took office on Jan. 8, 1887. In four months he was seized with a fatal illness, and died in the eighth month of his administration—the first Governor of California to die in office.

"He had barely entered upon the duties of his position and wearily forced himself through the labor of one legislative session before the shadow of impending dissolution fell upon him," his eulogists wrote, "and in official sense, he was practically withdrawn from public view" while for months "he was quietly and manfully battling against the insidious approach of fatal disease."[11]

Washington Bartlett left no direct heirs. He never was married. Biographers wrote of him that "although successful in business enterprises, he never allowed his fortune to accumulate beyond $100,000, nor his private expenses to exceed $200 per month—the excess was systematically devoted to charity and assisting relatives and friends."[12]

For a youth out of frontier Apalachicola and Tallahassee, Washington Bartlett went a long way. Florida's loss was California's gain.

NOTES

1. The material for this summary of the Life of Josiah Bartlett came from Allen Johnson, ed., *Dictionary of American Biography* (New York: Charles Scribner's Sons, 1929), 2:9-11.

2. The *National Cyclopaedia of American Biography* (New York: James T. White & Co., 1897), 4: 113 (hereafter cited as *American Biography*).

3. James Owen Knauss, *Territorial Florida Journalism* (DeLand, Florida: Florida State Historical Society, 1926), pp. 53-54.

4. Ibid., p. 54.

5. Ibid., p. 56.

6. Ibid., p. 54.

7. Ibid., pp. 55-56.

8. Ibid., p. 55.

9. Washington Bartlett's career as a journalist in pioneer California was compiled from *The Memorial of Life and Services of Washington Bartlett, Late Governor of the State of California* (San Francisco: Society of California Pioneers, 1888), pp. 20-22.

10. Ibid., p. 22.

11. Ibid., p. 6-7.

12. *American Biography*, 4:113.

Chapter Eleven

Lafayette -
Absentee Landlord

The Marquis de LaFayette, aristocratic French hero of the American war for independence, was probably the largest individual landowner of territorial middle Florida; but he never stepped foot on his acreage.

He probably never had any idea of occupying the township which ran to within a short walk of the territorial Capitol, though the developers of early Tallahassee hoped he would lend his prestigious name to their ambitious plans.

Lafayette chose (or had chosen for him) 24,000 acres at the northwestern boundary of Tallahassee after Congress in 1825 voted him a township of unclaimed land and $200,000 cash for his services nearly 50 years before in the American revolution. He needed the money to pay his debts after a career of riding the crest and sliding into the depths during the revolution, reign of terror and rise and fall of republics, dictatorships and monarchies which kept his homeland in tumult most of his life.

It was not surprising that Lafayette should choose his township in Florida and at Tallahassee. The Florida territory had only been taken over from Spain four years before. Tallahassee had just been selected for the capital and the surrounding land put up for sale. Planters and politicians from the older states were casting eyes at the new land. Lafayette was in Washington where "Florida" was beginning to have the magic sound of its first land boom.

Moreover, the general had fallen in with Richard Keith Call, Florida's first full term delegate to Congress who had been

among the very first Americans to take land at Tallahassee after
it was selected for the Capital. Call is credited with selling
Lafayette on the area. The aging hero also had been a friend of
George Walton, the Signer, whose son was secretary of the
Florida territory. And if he had come to see his Florida land
before he died, Lafayette would have run into acquaintances
aplenty, though they would have been a generation or two his
junior.

He would have recognized Catherine Willis Murat as one of
the two belles who held candelabra beside him on the balcony
where he had received the hero's welcome at Fredericksburg,
Virginia, only a few years before. (He may not have been so
enchanted with her husband, Achille Murat, nephew of Napoleon Bonaparte whose regime Lafayette had not admired. He
had helped depose Napoleon after the defeat at Waterloo.)

He could have had much to discuss with Francis Eppes,
grandson of Thomas Jefferson, a friend of decades standing who
as U.S. minister to France had helped Lafayette write a French
counterpart of the American Declaration of Independence
which Jefferson authored.[1] When Lafayette reached Richmond
on his American visit in 1825, the aged Jefferson had sent
young Eppes and another grandson, Thomas Jefferson
Randolph, to represent him at a reception in the Frenchman's
honor. Lafayette, in turn, visited Jefferson at Monticello for six
weeks. Eppes, who lived nearby, undoubtedly talked with
Lafayette—and perhaps about Florida, for the Florida fever was
burning throughout Virginia. Young Eppes had it, and made the
move within a year or two.

The French nobleman Marie Joseph Paul Yves Roch Gilbert
du Montier, Marquis de LaFayette, was only 19 years old but
already stirring with democratic convictions when the American
colonies rebelled against England. He had been trained for
military duties; so he offered his services to the American
revolution in December of 1776.

From Silas Dean, American agent in Paris, he won an
agreement that he should hold the rank of a major general in
the continental army. The struggling new American nation was
desperate for European recognition and aid. Its Declaration of
Independence was a forthright appeal for understanding from
"a candid world" grounded in conviction that "a decent respect
for the opinions of mankind" required a statement of causes for
separation from the mother country. The voluntary help of a

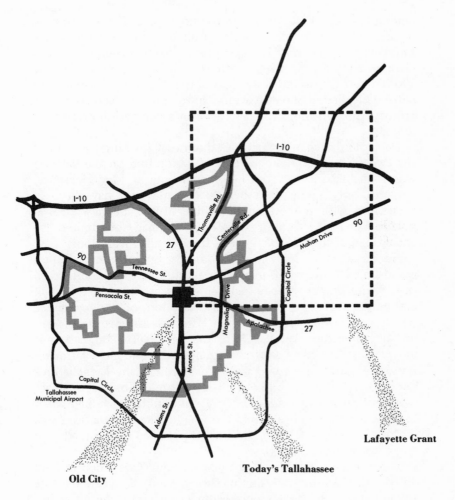

Lafayette Grant
French hero of American revolution once was major Florida landowner.

Lafayette in Virginia Campaign, 1781
Engraving by Noel LeMire from a painting by J. B. LePaon
U.S. Bureau of Ships National Archives

"Beauty lighted Valor to the front."

Lafayette at Fredericksburg
On tour of U.S. in 1824, escorted to balcony by Catherine Willis Gray
(later Mrs. Achille Murat) and her cousin, Mrs. Grey.

Sketch in undated clipping from Household Magazine.

popular French nobleman, even one still in his 'teens was a stroke of diplomatic recognition.

Young Lafayette was no armchair general. He joined the staff of George Washington as an aide and referred to him as his "adopted father." But he went into the ranks, too. He was wounded at the first Battle of Brandywine on September 11, 1777. He was given command of a division while he still was only 20. After all, his formal military training in France probably exceeded by far that of most native Americans in the rag-tag army of revolution.

Though he had to leave France secretly because his government disapproved of his venture in American Independence, Lafayette became a hero at home as well as in America—a symbol of democracy which was beginning to rise in the hearts of Frenchmen. The popular sentiment contributed to the French treaty of amity and commerce with the United States. When the first French contingents arrived, in 1778, he became liaison officer between the Americans and the French commander, the comte d'Estaing.

Later that year Lafayette returned to France where, at the request of Congress, he presented the Americans' needs to his government. When the continental army had its back to the wall in 1780, Lafayette returned to America with the bolstering news that an expeditionary force was on its way from France under General Rochambeau. Again, he was liaison between the two armies. In April, 1781, he was given command of the American army in Virginia and was involved in final defeat of the English at Yorktown.[2]

Lafayette earned his pay as a major general in the American army; but he didn't draw it. He paid his own expenses and contributed cash to the American cause—some were to say later that his losses exceeded $200,000.[3]

American independence won, Lafayette went home "the hero of two worlds" and in 1782 was given the same rank, major general, in the French army that he had held under Washington.

America didn't forget him. On a visit in 1784 he was given honorary citizenship in several states. He spoke, as if a citizen, in favor of a tighter union several years before the United States constitution was adopted.

Back in France, his fortunes rose and ebbed with the radical changes of government—from national leadership to political imprisonment, from wealth to poverty. Americans held steady in their gratitude. In 1794, Congress heard of his distress, and—with Jefferson's prodding—Lafayette was voted $24,424 for the "pay and emoluments of a major-general during the time he was in the service of the United States."[4] It didn't go far to clear the debts and expenses for deterioration of his properties while he had been a prisoner during the reign of terror following the French Revolution.

In 1803, Congress went to his aid again—this time granting him the right to take 11,520 acres of any unsettled land in the Northwest Territory. However, Jefferson got him permission to take the land in Louisiana, which Jefferson had recently purchased for the United States from France. Lafayette chose land near New Orleans, but a quick resale to help him out of his financial plight at home was frustrated by numerous claims that others had settled it ahead of him. Lafayette's friends said he was too reluctant to contest even the most unjustifiable claims. It was 20 years before he disposed of the Louisiana grant. By that time, he was broke again; and grateful Americans heard about it.[5]

Congress passed an act inviting the ailing and aging Lafayette to visit once more the nation he had helped in its most troubled infancy. The government even offered to send a ship for him. Lafayette hesitated. His debts were so heavy he couldn't walk away from them nor out from under them. Three friends in France—two Americans and a Dutchman—lent him enough to reduce them sufficiently to let him make the trip in 1824 with a clear conscience.[6]

He and his son, George Washington Lafayette, sailed by private vessel for America and a rousing reception the old hero did not expect. It had been 40 years since he last stepped on United States soil. Senator Thomas Hart Benton in his memoirs said the "enthusiasm of the young generation astonished and excited him and gave him a new view of himself—a future glimpse of himself—and such as he would be seen in after ages."[7] Lafayette was lionized everywhere he went.

Congress voted a new grant—$200,000 cash and a township of any unsettled land wherever he could find and choose it. The grant was approved four days before Christmas, 1824.[8] The first white settlers had just begun to arrive in the fertile old fields of Tallahassee.

The Territorial Legislative Council was holding its first session in the temporary log cabin Capitol, and already looking ahead. Only a week after the Lafayette grant was voted in Washington, the Council adopted a memorial to Congress declaring:

> That influenced by a confident belief, that the improvement and population of Florida is peculiarly a subject of national concern; That it is all important to the United States to strengthen a frontier, to which nature has assigned so large a portion of sea coast, and Agricultural resources; we need no additional encouragement to lay before Congress our views in relation to these objects.
>
> Your Memorialists on referring to the characters of the climate and topography of this Territory and considering its capacity for producing the orange, the olive and the vine, together with sugar and cotton and the more valuable tropical staples, cannot but lament that these resources should lay dormant and that objects of so much national wealth should be withheld from the industry and enterprise of the Citizens of the United States.
>
> This condition of the Territory your memorialists ascribe to the delay attendant on the adjustment of the land claims and the want of a legal and settled line of demarcation between public and private property. The planter cannot emigrate to Florida, because he cannot purchase lands with a clear legal title; the old inhabitants of the Territory are suffering under poverty and distress, and there is a general inactivity in Agriculture and a consequent depression in commerce and trade; all of which evils your memorialists are of opinion might in a great measure be removed by the interposition of Congress in terminating or modifying the system of investigating land claims, which seems to have been so ineffectual in producing an adjustment, And your memorialists would suggest whether it would not comport with justice and with the interest of the United States that such of the land claims as may be rejected or undecided by the land commissioners, may at the option of the individuals concerned be carried before the Superior Courts for decision and that Congress in its wisdom might give to the said commissioners such latitude in their operations as might afford more facility to the object of adjustment.[9]

What's more, the legislators said, Florida needed a canal across the state via the Suwannee and St. Johns rivers, and "the endowment of a Territorial University" by setting aside a township of land "in the Middle District" to be sold for its financing.[10]

Lafayette need look no further for his grant of land. He was touring the South, with popular receptions at Savannah, Mobile and New Orleans, where he took up headquarters.

President Monroe, through his Commissioner of U.S. Lands, George Graham, named Col. John McKee, an Alabama Congressman, to visit Tallahassee, select a suitable township for Lafayette and offer advice on the time and terms to sell. Lafayette had used $80,000 of his cash grant to pay debts and expenses, and had invested the remaining $120,000 in U.S. government bonds bearing 4 per cent interest.[11] So he wasn't hurting.

McKee arrived in Tallahassee in April, 1825, and quickly advised Graham that he recommended that Lafayette claim Township 1 North Range 1 East—running six miles due north from the meridian marker in what now is Cascades Park, then six miles east, six miles south and six miles west again to the meridian marker.

McKee complained mildly about the spring rains that had kept him from a thorough inspection of the land but, he reported on April 21, 1825, "if people can enjoy health here it is certainly the most delightful region I have ever seen."

However, he observed, "with all the advantages it offers you may expect to hear of but few spots selling above the minimum price."[12] The first auction sale of plantation lands had brought disappointing bids of only $1.25 an acre. Sale of town lots on 160 acres which was to become downtown Tallahassee raised only $45,000 to finance the territorial government and construct its necessary buildings. Graham sent McKee's report to Lafayette at New Orleans:

"You will perceive that he has selected 'a township' for you which adjoins the town of Tallahassee, this I presume is the most valuable township in Florida."[13] The warrant giving title to Lafayette was issued appropriately, on July 4, 1825—only one year short of the nation's 50th birthday.

Graham and McKee advised Lafayette not to sell too soon, but predicted in less than two years he should be able to realize $150,000 by disposing of his township. A year and a half later, Graham relayed to Richard Keith Call, receiver of funds for land sale, and Robert Butler, surveyor general, Lafayette's authorization to lay off 160 acres due east of the Capitol in 100 foot lots and offer them for sale. George Ward who, with Call had charge of Tallahassee land sales, months earlier had recommended subdividing the quarter-section for residential lots. He said he had examined the tract "as well as the thickets that cover it will permit and find it a valuable piece of land and think it certainly will afford convenience to the inhabitants of Tallahassee to have it sold out in the manner proposed, and I should suppose restricted as they are from using the timber on the reserves near town that it would bring a pretty fair price even at an early period, yet it seems most likely that it would bring more at the time of the next land sale (when it is expected there will be a great deal of money here) than at an earlier period. It lies adjoining Tallahassee . . . and the street running through the center of town Eastward [now Park avenue] will pass longitudinally through the center of this half section. . . ."[1][4]

There were complications. Before word of the congressional grant reached Tallahassee, Governor William P. Duval had built a house on part of the land given to Lafayette. He agreed to take equal acreage southeast of the Capitol (in the present Myers Park area) surrendering his claim to the Lafayette section to the north on condition that the government reimburse him for the cost of improvements. That claim was in the courts for several years, along with others.

Though Lafayette seems never to have thought of moving onto the Florida land himself—much to the disappointment of some who thought his prestigious presence would hasten development of the area—he did dream about successful plantation ventures on it.

After his return to France, he wrote to his friend Call:

> . . . It seems to me also that the introduction of the kine, mulberry, olive tree, silk worm, managed by experienced hands would prove a true service to the country. A difficulty in my opinion appears to arise from the unfitness of European labourers for that important part of the work, clearing the ground, how to manage it you know better than I can do. Don't you think sir, a prospect opens very favorable to the welfare of Florida? . . . But whatever the Southern states, under a climate, upon a soil with suitable free white, and upon the whole cheaper labour, can in that manner obtain additional wealth, strength, and population, I cannot think, why they should not continue the opportunity. Swarms of German labourers, now unprovided with money are embarking twice a month for New York. Here is another contemplated speculation. However productive of precious staples Florida may be, and cultivation of the vine, olive, and mulberry tree, and the silk worm would now be a desirable addition to her industry. I contemplate the

sale of part of my Township, perhaps it will induce you and your
friends if a new prospect opens to renew the former idea of a bargain
on the lands. . . .[15]

From this we may surmise that Lafayette, like Attorney
General William Wirt and others, had visions of plantations
operated by free colonies. He abhorred slavery. There was a
wave of interest in England and the United States about that
time for Utopian colonies such as the social reformer George
Owens had started at New Lanark in England and New
Harmony, Indiana.

Frances Wright, a wealthy English devotee of Owens'
schemes and a close friend of Lafayette, wanted to come to the
United States with him on his last visit, but the General's family
considered it improper. She came, though, on another boat and
was close to him on his tour. This may not have been a romantic
attachment. It was said she so admired Lafayette that she
wanted him to adopt her as a daughter. It is reasonable to think
that she had a dream to sell him concerning use of his Tallahassee
land for a cooperative colony. She actually financed one near
Memphis, Tennessee, herself but like Owens' utopia at New
Harmony it failed for lack of industry and enterprise by the
colonists.[16]

Lafayette turned down an offer of $50,000 for half his
township from Call, and tried to sell tracts to Frenchmen. A
small contingent of them arrived in 1831 and made a feeble
attempt to scratch a living out of small tracts while slave-owning
planters were farming hundreds of acres. Their vines didn't
produce. They found titles given in France were defective. Most
of them soon left. There is a recurrent tale that they moved into
Tallahassee and became merchants in the area long known as
Frenchtown. However, Dr. Dorothy Dodd, retired State librarian who has delved as deeply into Tallahassee history as anyone,
claims to have established by a work not yet published that few
if any of the French purchasers of Lafayette land stayed in
Tallahassee. She says the families of the Frenchtown area were
from a later immigration from France.

Lafayette died in Paris May 20, 1834, still holding some of
the Tallahassee land given him 10 years earlier. A year before he
had consented to sell three-fourths of it for $46,520, payable in
10 years, to three Tallahassee planters and investors.[17] They
wanted it not only for resale at a profit, but to begin
development of the huge tract which some thought was stifling

growth of the little capital city by standing idle at the very edge of town.

He needed the money again. But he wrote to friends: "I am determined in honor to the gift in compliance with my own feelings, to remain in possession of a part of the land. I had contemplated to retain several sections but will be content with one and a half, a little more than 300 acres for each of my children after me, provided that share is selected near the city on the most pleasant and promising spot."[18]

The late Kathryn Abbey Hanna calculated through examination of deeds that Lafayette and his heirs received about $103,000, over a period of more than 30 years of ownership.[19]

No Lafayettes ever occupied the grant, but in 1850, before the last piece was sold, two grandsons of the hero came to Tallahassee and were given public recognition exemplary of the gratitude Americans always must acknowledge to one whom Jefferson called the "doyen . . . of the soldiers of liberty of the world."[20] His name lives on the historic markers and street signs of Tallahassee, and the name of a little county 75 miles south of the gift of land he claimed but never saw.

NOTES

1. On July 11, 1789, Lafayette presented to the French National Assembly the "First European Declaration of the Rights of Man and of Citizens." It was the third draft of a political "catechism of France," which Lafayette had been revising since January. While it is likely but not documented that Jefferson assisted in the first draft, copies of the second draft contain marginal comments in Jefferson's own hand. Further the principles and language of the second draft are strongly suggestive of Jefferson's direct influence. In certain respects, Lafayette's third draft was a more conservative document and revised some of Jefferson's suggestions. The Assembly agreed that the constitution should contain a declaration of rights and appointed a committee to write the constitution. Lafayette was an alternate member. While numerous proposals from other sources were considered, Lafayette's third draft was clearly the principal model for the French bill of rights as finally adopted in August of 1789. The most complete American treatment of Lafayette's role in the Great French Revolution is Louis Gottschalk and Margaret Maddox, *Lafayette in the French Revolution Through the October Days* (Chicago: University of Chicago Press, 1969).

2. The material for this five-paragraph summary of Lafayette's contributions to the American Revolution came from the *Encyclopaedia Britannica* (Chicago: William Benton, 1972), 13:592-593.

3. Kathryn T. Abbey, "The Story of the Lafayette Lands in Florida," *The Florida Historical Society Quarterly* 10 (January 1932): 115 (hereafter cited as Abbey, "Lafayette"). Abbey's source for this figure is a

letter from Jefferson to Washington (December 31, 1793). French historians put Lafayette's losses at 700,000 livres with the purchasing power of the livre being roughly equivalent to the contemporary American dollar. See Louis Gottschalk, *Lafayette and the Close of the American Revolution* (Chicago: University of Chicago Press, 1942), p. 421.

4. Abbey, "Lafayette," pp. 116-117.

5. Ibid., pp. 117-118.

6. The loan came from "James Brown, American minister to France; a Dutchman whose name was Kock; and James Francois Girod, a citizen of New Orleans, who was at that time in France." William E. Woodward, *Lafayette* (New York: Farrar & Rinehart, Inc., 1938), p. 417 (hereafter cited as Woodward, *Lafayette*).

7. Thomas Hart Benton, *Thirty Years View: or A History of the Working of the American Government for Thirty Years From 1820 to 1850*, 2 vols. (New York: D. Appleton and Co., 1854), 1:30.

8. Abbey, "Lafayette," p. 120. The bills for compensation encountered difficulties in both House and Senate. Strongly supported by Senator Hayne and Congressman McDuffie (both from South Carolina), the Senate bill passed 38 to 7 and the House voted 166 to 26 in favor of its bill. The consensus of opposition seemed not to have been directed at Lafayette personally, but was a question of policy.

9. Clarence E. Carter, ed., *The Territorial Papers of the United States*, 27 vols. (Washington, D.C.: The United States Government Printing Office, 1958), 23:135-136 (hereafter cited as Carter, *Territorial Papers*).

10. Ibid., pp. 136-137.

11. Abbey, "Lafayette," p. 122. Woodward, *Lafayette*, p. 428. Quite typical of Lafayette's generous nature, he offered to pay off President Monroe's debts. Monroe, of course, refused and suggested the purchase of government bonds.

12. Carter, *Territorial Papers*, 23:238.

13. Ibid., 23:272.

14. Ibid., 23: 347.

15. Richard Keith Call, "Journal of Richard Keith Call," manuscript copy in possession of Mrs. LeRoy Collins, Tallahassee, Florida, pp. 272-274.

16. Woodward, Lafayette, pp. 412-415, 418, 433. Also Gorton Carruth, ed., *The Encyclopedia of American Facts and Dates* (New York: Thomas Y. Growell, 1959), 1:62.

17. Abbey, "Lafayette," p. 130.

18. Ibid., p. 129.

19. Ibid., p. 133.

20. *Encyclopaedia Britannica* (Chicago: William Benton, 1972), 13:593.

Chapter Twelve

Florida's Whites

Joseph M. White must have been the most popular politician of Florida's territorial period, though his wife, the gracious "Florida" White, has been more glamorized in history and pseudo-history.

Mary Ellen Adair White was nicknamed "Florida" in Washington when her husband went to Congress in 1825. The name stuck as she moved through the high circles of society in the United States and abroad.

It is hard to separate the careers of Joe and Florida White. She seems to have participated actively in his campaigns (though she sickened of the bitterness at one point and yearned for diplomatic service). His critics were influential by appointment from Washington, but were beaten by White every time they challenged him in popular election. They tended to give his wife credit for his success—perhaps as much to cover their own embarrassment as to acknowledge her charms.

Mary Ellen Adair White was one of seven daughters, all belles by reputation, of John Adair of Kentucky—revolutionary soldier, Indian fighter, Governor of Kentucky, member of the U.S. Senate and House of Representatives. He was born in South Carolina and was a member of the convention which ratified the United States Constitution for his native state. He moved to territorial Kentucky and was a member of the convention which wrote Kentucky's state constitution. Mary Ellen was born to politics and grew up with it.[1]

Joseph M. White was born in Franklin County, Kentucky in 1781.[2] He studied law and had been well established there as an attorney and prosecutor before he married Ellen when she was

95

scarcely half his age. He was ambitious, and ready to move westward or southward as the American frontier advanced in either direction from Kentucky. He unsuccessfully applied for presidential appointment to the territorial legislatures of Alabama and Missouri before Florida was acquired from Spain.

President Monroe named him to Florida's first legislative council in 1822. White said in his application he wanted the assignment because of his wife's delicate health.[3]

They arrived at Pensacola in the same conveyance which brought William P. Duval, another Kentuckian, to take up his duties as the first civil governor of the Territory of Florida. From that moment, Duval and White careers coincided; though they didn't always mesh politically.

White didn't stay in the legislative council much longer than he was needed to provide a quorum for its first session in Pensacola—when five of the 13 members never got there and yellow fever took the life of the presiding officer.

Before the fragment of legislature gathered, White already had received judicial appointment as acting U.S. Attorney for West Florida upon the death of the first man commissioned, Tipton B. Harrison, who had come down from Lynchburg, Va., and hardly settled in the position when he was stricken.[4]

Though White had submitted his resignation from the legislature when he took up his duties as acting U.S. Attorney, he agreed to postpone it in order to help organize the council.[5] Formalities had to be compromised freely in those days when there were only a handful of Americans in old Spanish Florida, when all orders and commissions had to come by slow mail or courier from Washington—and when some who were appointed didn't arrive at all or soon fell victims to disease or disaster. Being healthy and available was an asset for success. Joseph White was both, in addition to being capable.

Though the U.S. attorneyship paid more than membership in the legislature, one of the most lucrative jobs in the territory was membership on the commission established to settle the old Spanish land claim disputes the United States assumed when it acquired Florida. This was White's dish, but Monroe had named three others. One never showed up; another soon resigned. The remaining Commissioner, Samuel R. Overton, pleaded with the President to fill the vacancies so he could get on with clearing up the land titles. "The United States are greatly interested in expediting the business of the commissioners, so as to bring it

Mary Ellen Adair White
belle of Casa Bianca
and Washington Society

Portrait painted from a miniature.

to an early close, and enable them speedily to expose their lands to sale," Overton said in a letter dated July 10, 1823, more than a year after American occupation of the territory. Besides, he said:

"to continue here during the Summer and Fall, exposed to the diseases incident to those seasons in this climate, without any prospect of forming a Board, is a delay which is extremely discouraging and painful, and from which I should be much pleased to be relieved."

He urged appointment of White:

Mr. Joseph M. White of this place, has been repeatedly pressed upon your attention, as better qualified to fill either of those vacancies, than any individual who can be selected. He is a gentleman in whom the people here repose every confidence, and his appointment, I am assured, would meet with universal approbation. He was recommended because he was known to you, and from a consciousness of his qualifications. A regard to the interests of the claimants and the United States, again constrain me to urge the appointment of Mr. White to fill the first vacancy that is presented. It is particularly desirable as it respects the speedy and faithful execution of our duties. If two new members of the Board join me, who are unacquainted with the laws and ordinances of Spain etc. and the distribution of lands, almost the whole burthen, at this stage of the business, will be thrown upon me. This is more than my present state of health would bear, impaired as it has been by the irregularities and inclemency of the past seasons. With the aid of Mr. White, who is well acquainted with the duties to be performed, we could proceed with but little difficulty. No delay could arise, as he is on the spot, and the whole business could be taken up and dispatched with fidelity and promptitude.[6]

White already had been appointed to the Commission a couple of weeks before, on June 26; but his notification didn't reach Pensacola until two weeks after Overton had undertaken to nudge the President into action.

Though the long delay frustrated the claims board, and it couldn't complete its review of claims before expiration of the commission's term, White distinguished himself as an authority on the subject. He wrote a classic two-volume work, published in 1839, called: "*A New Collection of Laws, Charters, etc. of Great Britain, France and Spain Relating to Cessions of Lands, with the Laws of Mexico.*"[7] Attorney General William Wirt and Daniel Webster discussed at one time employing him as special attorney to represent the nation in later litigation over land claims in new territories. There is little indication that White found the proposition attractive.

When the capital moved to Middle Florida, the Whites moved

with it to a planatation in Jefferson county about 25 miles east of Tallahassee. Appropriately, they named it Casa Bianca (White house).[8] It became the political home base for his 12 years as Florida's lone delegate to the U.S. House of Representatives.

At Casa Bianca, the stately "Florida" White was in charge. At the age of 28, a passport application said she was five feet, seven inches tall, with black hair and eyes.[9] "The Queens of American Society," published in 1867, said "she was a fasionable belle in Washington for several years, and was celebrated for her magnificent person and her accomplishments throughout the Gulf states. She spent some time in Europe."[10]

Ellen's sister, Mrs. Benjamin F. Pleasants, also was "much admired in Washington society, and took an interest in public affairs."[11] Their cousin Susan Fitzhugh, widowed at 17, put them in the shade, however, when Ellen White brought her to the Capital. The author of the "Queens" said Mrs. Fitzhugh at home in Louisville was "esteemed as one of the brightest ornaments of Western society." ("West" in those days, meant from west of the Appalachians.)

At Washington under Florida White's sponsorship, Cousin Susan "became a courted belle in the fashionable world. Her beauty was its blooming perfection. Her form was tall and exquisitely proportioned. She possessed a commanding dignity of mien, with faultless grace in every movement. . . . Her voice was musical, and she had a fascinating eloquence in conversation. The elegance of high-breeding in her was harmonious with her feminine gentleness, and her playful humor gave her still more powerful attractions."[12] Her daughter by her first husband married a nephew of President James K. Polk. The widowed Susan married a U.S. land officer commissioner who soon became a federal judge.

So, by personal attractions and reflected fascination from beauteous kinship, Florida White moved well in Washington society where her husband, being only a territorial delegate, had a voice but not a vote in national politics.

Back home in Florida, Ellen White was no less a star. Ellen Call Long, who as a child knew her personally, wrote in her memoirs, "Florida Breezes," that White had "a pillar of strength in his wife . . . a very accomplished woman of great tact; they have no children, which makes a difference."[13]

She recalled Mrs. White and her sister, Mrs. Pleasants, at the races in Tallahassee:

both brilliant conversationalists, vast tact, and of fine personal appearance; and they are here (they say) to electioneer for the suffrage of the people, in behalf of the incumbent (White) who remains at his post in Washington; while these two young ladies, accompanied by one or more young men of the territory, have canvassed every county in the interest of the absent candidate, much to his advantage, as Mrs. White is said to be the cleverest of the two.[14]

At another point in her book, Mrs. Long called Ellen White:

A spendid looking woman, in full maturity. A wild girl of the West, transformed into a woman of the world, the force of the first in no degree lessened, with much added thereunto. Acquaintance with national society as displayed at Washington City, together with a foreign sojourn, has illuminated a high natural intelligence, by information and experience.

While some women are best at tete-a-tete, Mrs. White entertains numbers, giving always preference to the society of gentlemen, who, while they yielded admiration, gave more latitude to subject and speech on her part. . . .

Her adaptiveness to electioneering is said to be wonderful, and that most of his (White's) success is owing to this fact.[15]

As for Delegate White, Mrs. Long was deprecating:

Colonel White has friends that think he can do no wrong; there are others slow to believe good of him. A man that will do all the good he can for his friends, and all the harm possible to his enemies, has rather a fascination for me, but I do not think from what I can learn that this is the policy of Colonel White, he rather treats one as if he expected him to be the other on any emergency, he thinks little of the gratitude of men; he builds more security upon their interests; neither virtue or vice influence him. Special usefulness to him is the question. He talks well on the spirit of the times, and generalizes without offence, and plays his part so well that in one portion of the territory he boasts of being in favor with the administration, and in another he passes for a State's rights man.[16]

If you detect a tone of distinct dislike in Mrs. Long's appraisal of Delegate White, and a tint of cattiness about his attractive wife, remember the author held a bias:

Joseph White ousted her father, Richard Keith Call, from Congress after only one term, then beat Call's friend James Gadsden four times and Call once more in their effort to capture the only position subject to statewide popular vote in territorial Florida. Call and White were rivals from the very beginning. Both had been active candidates for the U.S.

Attorney job at Pensacola when the territorial government was set up in 1822. White got it when the first appointee, Tipton Harrison, soon died.

"We are personal enemies," Call said bluntly in an 1827 letter accusing White of being behind an anonymous letter to the Secretary of the Treasury questioning his integrity as receiver of funds for sale of public lands at Tallahassee. "I know him to be capable of such an act," Call said of White.[17]

The official territorial papers hardly bear out Ellen Call Long's estimate of Delegate Joe White as one who would straddle a fence for political expedience.

He slashed at red tape even before he was well launched on his career in Florida. When payment was slow coming for his services as acting U.S. Attorney at Pensacola, he sent the Treasury Department a curt note reminding that "it may not be a great deal of trouble, at the department to condemn bills for informality, but the department should not be converted into the scrupulous formality of a merchant ship and put officers at the distance of 1,000 miles to such expense, mortification and trouble."[18]

Another time he wrote to Washington observing "I discover that the government does not display the same alacrity in paying as collecting money.[19]

He took on the high and the low—

He complained to members of Andrew Jackson's cabinet that the President was following the advice of his defeated opponents more than his in making appointments in Florida.

He asked President John Quincy Adams to replace Governor Duval with a man of commanding reputation in order to relieve contentiousness in Florida, and to exercise care in selection of other officers. He complained to President Jackson in March 1834 about Duval's long absences from the territory and suggested that "if the President will stop his salary during his absence I will venture to say he will not go. I entreat in the name of the people of Florida that he (Duval) be required to remain there as long as he holds office; and take(s) the salary."[20] It was only a few weeks until Jackson replaced Duval before the end of his term with Governor John Eaton.

Delegate White also was quick to report political activity adverse to him, and favoring Gadsden, by employes working on government projects—but Jackson paid little attention, apparently.

However, though such political give and take sprinkles through much of the record, White seems to have gone seriously about the territory's business. He pressed successfully for improved lighthouses at St. Marks and St. Joseph. He pushed road construction and won congressional backing for the beginning of an inland waterway system down the entire Florida east coast, and from the Apalachicola to the Choctawhatchee on the upper west coast.

He was a prime mover in getting a survey as early as 1826 for a canal across the state linking the Suwannee and St. Johns rivers.

His constant rival, Gadsden, got the job of directing the survey, and White complained at least one of the surveyors was going around saying it never would be dug unless the people ousted White and sent Gadsden to Congress. (The people didn't, and, sure enough, the canal hasn't been finished—but that's an unending story.)

White also worked for popular election of more officials in Florida, and he got Congress to pass a bill providing for every county to have a member of the territorial legislature, raising the representation from 13 members (sometimes from outside the state) appointed by the President.

He spoke out successfully for the pre-emption law which allowed small settlers to hold their lands against big buyers and syndicates when public land was put up for sale at auction.

He wrote the U.S. Commissioners of lands in 1825, regarding land sales in the Chipola district:

> It is certainly the interest as well as the duty of government in a frontier and exposed country, to sell out their lands to small settlers where they can get a fair price, rather than to large planters who would quarter the borders of the Union with overseers and Negroes.[21]

Such an attitude would not endear him to the big planters and land speculators.

White stayed in Congress through the presidential administrations of John Quincy Adams, the two tumultuous terms of Andrew Jackson and into the time of Martin Van Buren. He whipped Gadsden one more time in 1835, then decided to retire from politics to enter business and pick up his law practice.[22]

This probably pleased his wife, Ellen. Despite her reputation as an astute politician and campaigner for her husband, she had early in the game tried to get him out of politics and into the diplomatic service. In the Memoirs of John Quincy Adams there is a notation on a paper dated January 27, 1827, which says:

> J. M. White wishes to be appointed Charge d'Affairs to Denmark. Mrs. White very unwilling to go back to Florida. He has no doubt of his own re-election, but must fight his way there. Barely escaped a duel the last time he was there.[23]

Nevertheless, White didn't get into the foreign service. He was re-elected again and again. Ellen seems to have taken to the Florida life. The Florida State Library has a batch of water colors of native flowers (some not bad) credited to her.

White died during a business trip to St. Louis two years after he left Congress. Ellen, the glamorous "Florida" a widow in her middle thirties, met an Irish gentleman named Theophilus Beattie on a trip to New Orleans, married him and returned to Florida to live beyond the bounds of politics.[24]

Beattie died after about five years. Ellen sold Casa Bianca and moved around to several southern cities before she died in Oxford, Miss., in 1884. She was 83 years old and in poor financial condition. Her grave is marked by a small stone which says only: "E.A.B." Ellen Adair Beattie.

NOTES

1. *Biographical Directory of the American Congress 1774-1961* (Washington, D.C.: United States Government Printing Office, 1961), pp. 457-458 (hereafter cited as *Biographical Directory*).
2. Ibid., p. 1805.
3. Clarence E. Carter, ed., *The Territorial Papers of the United States*, 27 vols. (Washington, D.C.: United States Government Printing Office, 1956), 22: 406, 423.
4. Ibid., 22:652.
5. Ibid., 22:537.
6. Ibid., 22:717-718.
7. *Biographical Directory*, p. 1805.
8. Ellen Call Long, *Florida Breezes or Florida New and Old* (Gainesville: University of Florida Press, 1962), p. 171 (hereafter cited as Long, *Florida Breezes*).
9. Her husband's passport at the same time (June 3, 1833) said he stood five feet, eleven inches and was bald. The passport also said he was 35 years old, though other records indicate he must have been 52.
10. Mrs. Elizabeth Fries (Lummis) Ellet, *The Queens of American Society* (Philadelphia: Porter & Coates, 1867), p. 225 (hereafter cited as Ellet, *Queens*).
11. Ibid., p. 226.
12. Ibid., p. 223-224.
13. Long, *Florida Breezes*, p. 143.
14. Ibid., p. 100.
15. Ibid., pp. 171-172.

16. Ibid., p. 171.
17. Carter, *Territorial Papers*, 23:798.
18. Ibid., 22:595.
19. Ibid., 23:47.
20. Ibid., 24:992-993. Earlier in Duval's twelve-year tenure, Congress had passed an act requiring territorial governors to get presidential permission before leaving their territories, but it was repealed a year later. Duval, notorious for his long absences at the beginning, seems to have slipped back into the habit toward the last.
21. Ibid., 23:371.
22. Gadsden ran third, behind William Wyatt, another perennial candidate. White had a majority over all three of his opponents.
23. Carter, *Territorial Papers*, 23:786.
24. Ellet, *Queens*, p. 225.

Chapter Thirteen

Peggy O'Neal's
Florida Interlude

There was no red, white and blue blood in the veins of Peggy O'Neale Eaton, but there was so much political tumult in her life that she must have a place in any collection of vignettes of territorial Florida society and government.

She tore Washington apart as no woman or man, before or since. She lasted less long as the first lady of Florida. History is confused on her reception in the frontier capital of Tallahassee; but by no account—including her own—did she find in Tallahassee the maelstrom she left in Washington.

The story has been told in song ("Peggy O'Neale, the girl who could steal any heart any place, any time") and in fiction, ("The Gorgeous Hussy"—made into a movie with Joan Crawford in the title role) and by numerous books and chapters of books—both scholarly and pseudo-history.

Peggy was real (though she wrote in her autobiography that nobody ever really called her "Peggy"). She was born Margaret O'Neale at Washington, in 1799, a year before the government was moved to the new national capital; so she and Washington society grew out of infancy together.[1] Her father and mother ran a tavern which soon became a boarding house, the Franklin House, and eventually a sort of hotel.

Peggy and her two sisters grew from childhood among her parents' boarders—on the knee of Vice President George Clinton, at the table with Andrew Jackson, in the confidence of Taney, Webster, Clay, and others of the political hierachy in the first two decades of the nineteenth century. Peggy was sent to

Peggy O'Neil   Claribel B. Jett

Andrew Jackson's Cabinet broke up in dispute over Peggy O'Neale Eaton.
Sketch by Claribel Jett from descriptions of Peggy O'Neale as a young
woman.

school in New York with the elite, but came home to manage her father's tavern. It was no low-grade place. Mr. and Mrs. James Monroe, on the way to the presidency, lived next door. The Capitol was just down the street.

After the British burned the government buildings in 1814, O'Neale's place served temporarily as offices for the U.S. Treasury. Before and after that the clientele at the hotel and its dining and wining facilities were the highest placed men in the nation's government. Most of them had left their wives and families at home for lack of facilities in the muddy new national capital. Peggy grew up among politicians, developed her charms and her interests among them. One biographer called her "Democracy's Mistress" although her morality had as many defenders as detractors. Though there was much talk of her indiscretions, none implied promiscuity.

At the age of 17 she married John B. Timberlake, a navy lieutenant with the lucrative commission as purser which allowed him to operate for profit the ship stores on U.S. naval vessels. To them were born two little girls before Lt. Timberlake died aboard the U.S. Constitution enroute from Greece to Italy. Peggy received word of her widowhood, and the consolation from her husband's friend, Sen. John Eaton of Tennessee, a boarder at the Franklin House and admirer of the young couple.

In time (critics maintained too little time) Peggy O'Neale Timberlake became Mrs. John Eaton. Despite the buzz of scandal in the capital town, incoming President Andrew Jackson made Eaton his Secretary of War. The buzz grew into a roar which in two years so preoccupied the administration that it became necessary for the entire Jackson cabinet (including the Secretary of War) to be replaced in order to settle down the government.

Peggy was the crux of the trouble although she and her defenders took the position that she was made the whipping girl to destroy her husband, who was among Jackson's most trusted advisers. Vice President John C. Calhoun and Secretary of State Martin Van Buren, both angling to be Jackson's successor, were blamed as devil's machinists in various versions. Peggy blamed Calhoun, who fell out with Jackson over much more significant differences.[2]

John Henry Eaton was born in 1790 in the Halifax district of North Carolina which sent many early settlers to territorial middle Florida. He moved northwestward into Tennessee and

became a power in that state's politics. He served with Andrew
Jackson in the War of 1812, became his first biographer,
campaign manager and loyal confidante.[3]

He and Jackson together had lived in the Franklin House
when both were senators from Tennessee. Both were fond of
Peggy. So was Jackson's wife, who lived there for a while. Eaton
was a wealthy widower, and you can get an argument 150 years
later on whether his fondness for Peggy became an amorous
affair before or after her husband died at sea. Enough vicious
and malicious gossip was current in Washington at the time to
cause such old friends of Jackson as Richard Keith Call of
Tallahassee to warn him against appointing the husband of
Peggy O'Neale Timberlake Eaton to his cabinet. The unsolicited
advice only lost Call favor with Jackson, who reminded the
Floridian that a tearful Peggy once had told him of having to
ward off Call's advances with a poke of the fire tongs.

Jackson appointed Eaton despite the scandal, and let it be
known he expected the members of his cabinet and their wives
to recognize Peggy socially. Van Buren, who had no wife, did;
but most of the others refused. Mrs. Calhoun and Mrs. John
Branch, wife of the Secretary of the Navy, seemed especially
recalcitrant. The Secretary of War and the Secretary of the
Navy stopped speaking.[4] Peggy held her chin up and attended
some parties where she was the belle of the evening—there being
few other women present. Undoubtedly she found some
pleasure in this situation, for she was at home among men, well
schooled in their political talk and more congenial than she
would have been among critical ladies in their drawing room.

The story has been told, retold, romanticized, distorted
and garbled. However, after two years, the whole cabinet
resigned or was fired by Jackson, stubborn by nature and
extremely loyal to Peggy. Eaton also resigned on April 21,
1831. (Some biographers suggest Van Buren slyly persuaded
him they should quit together for the good of the presidency.)

Calhoun had been elected vice president, so Jackson couldn't
fire him. However, he resigned—perhaps because he wanted to
run unattached for President, and undoubtedly because Jackson
had blown up in anger upon learning belatedly that Calhoun, as
Secretary of War, once had suggested a court martial for
Jackson over the 1818 foray into Spanish Florida when Jackson
ordered the execution of the British traders, Ambrister and
Arbuthnot, at St. Marks.[5] The whole episode was rehashed in

John H. Eaton
1790-1856
U.S. Senator, Secretary
of War, Governor
of Florida

*Dictionary of American
Portraits*

Peggy O'Neale Eaton
in her mature years

Henry Inman portrait from Pollack's Peggy
Eaton, Menton 1931

FSU Photo Archives

the press and in Congress. Moreover, Jackson and Calhoun collided head-on over state's rights—Calhoun insisting a state could nullify federal laws objectionable to it; Jackson adamant to the contrary. On such an issue, social recognition of Peggy Eaton must have been a minor provocation.

John and Peggy Eaton went back to Tennessee; but he retained his Washington interests, which included presidency of the Chesapeake and Ohio canal.[6] Van Buren became minister to Great Britain.

In 1832, Jackson was re-elected, with Van Buren as his vice president instead of Calhoun.

The new term began March 4, 1833. Six weeks later Jackson appointed Eaton Governor of Florida. It was a political surprise. Governor Duval had a year to serve on his term, and no resignation has been found in the records.[7] Furthermore, it was hardly a political plum for the wealthy Eaton to be shuffled off to the frontier of Florida, less than ten years raised out of the wilderness.

Peggy explained in her autobiography (written in her old age and published a century after the Jackson cabinet breakup) that "my health seemed to require another climate, and Mr. Eaton accepted the governorship of Florida, where he owned lands which he had previously purchased."[8]

There is more legend than recorded fact about Peggy Eaton's interlude in Florida or, for that matter, the administration of her husband as governor of the territory. Gaps in the published official territorial papers indicate he may not have been actually in Florida much more than half of his two-year term. His wife and her two children probably weren't in Tallahassee a full year all told. The record tends to confirm handed-down tales from old Tallahasseeans that her welcome wasn't warm enough, nor the facilities comfortable enough to hold her long and she found Pensacola more to her liking.

Though Eaton was appointed Governor in April of 1834, he was still in Washington in August, claiming his pay as Governor only from July 1. The family reportedly arrived in Tallahassee late in September of 1834. It is clear that Eaton wasn't in the capital at all during the final half of 1835, for there is a full six-month file of executive orders from July 1, 1835 to January 1, 1836 signed by G. K. Walker, territorial secretary, as "acting governor." Eaton was on the scene again with the New Year, but off for Washington and Spain in three and a half months.

He testily argued with the U.S. Comptroller over some
questioning of salary due him for the first part of 1836: ". . . I
was not dead—had not been removed, nor had resigned."[9] He
received his check.

Peggy, in her old-age biography, and some latter day
defenders have tried to make it appear she was warmly received
in Tallahassee. (No doubt she was, in part. One story is that a
reception for the new Governor and his wife in the Capitol
attracted every man who could get there—but not a single
woman.)

"We resided in Florida two years. They were beautiful years
to me," Peggy wrote 39 years later. "My neighbors were
pleasant. I had no ugly passages in my history, and I was away
from my husband's political persecutors."[10]

She seemed to emphasize the point, later averring:

> . . . in Florida our residence of course was at Tallahassee, the
> capital, to which he took us from Pensacola as soon as he could
> make the necessary arrangements. We had two happy years in
> Florida. To me it was the land of flowers as Washington had been
> the land of briars.[11]

She related an incident of their welcome in Tallahassee in
which it took all night to fire a 13-gun salute to the Governor at
an old fort with a "superannuated gun, which had not been
fired in a generation probably."[12] (John Lee Williams in "A
View of West Florida," published in 1827, said the muzzle of a
cannon found in the 1704 ruins of Fort San Luis had been
brought into Tallahassee and was fired on festive occasions.)

Leon Phillips in "That Eaton Woman," published in 1974,
enthralls us with this passage:

> In spite of its rural nature . . . Tallahassee boasted a number of
> magnificent homes. The most elegant being the Governor's Mansion,
> which sat at the center of a 12-acre site. It had more than 30 rooms,
> formal and informal gardens, its own extensive kitchen gardens, and
> a small lake that could be used for bathing. More than 40 servants
> were on the staff and lived in quarters behind the main house. All
> were slaves. . . .[13]

Phillips also gave Florida "a large handsomely appointed
Governor's Mansion" at Pensacola "and Governor Eaton was
expected to spend some portion of his time there, particularly
when the legislature was not in session."[14]

All that is sheer fabrication, embroidered and hemstitched.
Florida didn't provide a house for its governors anywhere until

1906, and modern governors must get by with a house half the
size of the fictitious mansion. It sits on a two-acre lot (no lake).

There never has been such a house, public or private, in
Tallahassee. If Eaton had been provided one, he would have
worked at home, for on April 2, 1835, he complained to the
Secretary of the Treasury about the sparseness of his quarters in
the Capitol:

> The office is without the comforts which should belong to it. A
> few chairs, some stained (painted) desks and an old pine table, make
> up its catalog of furniture, there are no curtains to the windows, no
> settees as you have in the City and no decent cases in which to
> preserve the books and records of the office and no carpet to the
> floor.[15]

Another time he complained about having no clerk or porter
to sweep out the office and go for the mail.

There may be as much or more truth in a quip former
students attribute to the late Weymouth T. Jordan, history
professor at Florida State University. He said Peggy found the
only decent houses in Tallahassee were on Calhoun street and
she refused to have that name in her address, so she moved to
Pensacola.

As a matter of fact, as other contemporary accounts in earlier
chapters of this book testify, most of the housing in Tallahassee
of territorial days was crude and temporary. A visitor in 1841
wrote home to the north that there wasn't a dwelling in the
town as handsome as his father's barn. That was five years after
the Eatons left.[16]

Phillips also has Peggy becoming very friendly with Richard
Call's wife, Mary—notably refraining, of course, from
mentioning the fire-tong rebuff of Mary's husband back in the
old Franklin House at Washington.

The two may have, indeed, gotten along all right in
Tallahassee, social amenities and politics being what they
are—and Call being out of the same old military and political
camp with Eaton. However, Mary Call's daughter, Ellen Call
Long, who was 10- and 11-years-old when the Eatons were in
Florida, mentioned no such relationship in her romanticized
memoirs, "Florida Breezes." Rather, she brushes off Peggy
Eaton with a paragraph about the scene at the Tallahassee race
track:

> In green velvet, with long flowing white plumes, was the new
> Governor's wife . . . and here, as elsewhere, she was surrounded by

admirers, but these all gentlemen . . . . If ugliness existed anywhere, it was hidden by the sure polish of success, and she was, as ever, replete in fascination; though she confesses not to like the social atmosphere here . . . . Governor Eaton will make Pensacola the home of his family.[17]

He may have done that; for when he got ready to leave Tallahassee on April 12, 1836, he wrote to President Jackson:

Tomorrow I shall leave this place, join my family which is at Pensacola, & by the way of N. Orleans proceed to Nashville. I should have replyed to yr letter of the 18 March earlier; but it came here during the time, I had made a flying visit to Pensacola. All my matters of arrangement public & private, being closed, there remains nothing to detain me longer in the Territory.

You remark in your letter, that I had 'expressed some astonishment at Calls nomination being made before I was confirmed' I beg to say that you misconceived me entirely . . . I only suggested that some difficulty might arise, with others (not myself for as you remark, I had not intended, under any state of things again to return to Florida. What I thought I foresaw would happen, did happen and but for my forebearance, something of serious import might have come of it. When I see you, I will inform you of the little outlines I would do so now, but it is not of value & importance sufficient to be written about.[18]

Whether or not he was constantly on the job in Tallahassee, Eaton didn't make much of a mark as Governor of Florida. The major event of his administration was the beginning of the Seminole Indian war, with the Dade massacre, and panic from settlers on the frontier. Frantic appeals for the militia to be called up went to the secretary and acting governor. Eaton was elsewhere.

On January 14, 1836, James Gadsden, Eaton's old friend and comrade in arms, politically as well as military, screwed up his courage and put his career in jeopardy to complain to their volatile commander:

We are literally without a government; without concert of action, or receprocity of good feeling, a universal distrust seems to pervade the whole community—without those who are officially cloathed with power acting in concert, all seem distracted in the general cry of something must be done, while all oppose every measure which can be suggested— We are literally like a ship tossed on the angry waves of the Ocean, without a helm, the Mariner asleep, and the crew divided among themselves. . . .[19]

So, exit John and Peggy Eaton. Within three months, Jackson recalled them and sent them off to Spain—and installed his old aide of the first days of the American takeover, Richard Keith Call.

Dictionary of American Portraits

Peggy Eaton, pert in old age.

EPILOG:

Eaton died in 1856. Peggy went into seclusion for a few years. Then in 1860 she married an Italian dancing teacher less than half her age. He hocked her silver, took her money, eloped with her favorite granddaughter and presented her with a greatgrandchild before she divorced him. She died in 1879, and is buried in Tennessee beside her second husband, John Henry Eaton, second civil governor of the territory of Florida.

NOTES

1. There are various spellings of Peggy's maiden name (O'Neal, O'Neil, O'Neille). I have chosen to utilize O'Neale because it seemed most popular. Controversy also exists about her birthdate. In her autobiography, the date given is 1799. The author has assumed that a lady is entitled to choose her own birthdate.

2. Unless otherwise noted, the material for this chapter came from Leon Phillips, *That Eaton Woman: In Defense of Peggy O'Neale Eaton* (New York: Crown publishers, 1974) (hereafter cited as Phillips, *Eaton Woman*).

3. *Webster's Biographical Dictionary* (Springfield, Massachusetts: G. G. Merriam Co., 1964), p. 461.

4. After the Eatons left Florida, Branch became Governor. (Call served two terms in between.) Mrs. Susan Bradford Eppes, Branch's granddaughter, recalled hearing Branch say that Jackson told him he was Jackson's choice to succeed him in office. At their final conference Jackson said, "You have now lost the Presidency." Branch replied, "But I have retained my honor."

5. Calhoun was the first vice president to resign. The only other to do so was Spiro T. Agnew.

6. Clarence E. Carter, ed., *The Territorial Papers of the United States*, 27 vols. (Washington, D.C.: United States Government Printing Office, 1960), 25:167 (hereafter cited as Carter, *Territorial Papers*).

7. Ibid., 25:3.

8. Margaret Eaton, *The Autobiography of Peggy Eaton* (New York: Charles Scribner's Sons, 1932), p. 170 (hereafter cited as Eaton, *Autobiography*).

9. Carter, *Territorial Papers*, 25:319.

10. Eaton, *Autobiography*, p. 170.

11. Ibid., pp. 173-174.

12. Ibid., p. 170.

13. Phillips, *Eaton Woman*, pp. 136-137.

14. Ibid., p. 139.

15. Carter, *Territorial Papers*, 25:158.

16. Dorothy Dodd, "Old Tallahassee," *Apalachee* (1957-1962): 67.

17. Ellen Call Long, *Florida Breezes: or Florida, New and Old* (Gainesville: University of Florida Press, 1962), pp. 99-100.

18. Carter, *Territorial Papers*, 25:272-273. The author has corrected spelling and punctuation.

19. Ibid., 25:224.

Chapter Fourteen

Hamilton Jr.,
and Shades of Burr

Alexander Hamilton, Jr., may not have reckoned, when he took a government job in the brand new territory of Florida, that he would have to work with a follower of the man who killed his father. There is no record that it bothered him much.

Young Hamilton was the first United States attorney for East Florida, appointed by President Monroe on April 15, 1822.[1] He was the second son of Alexander Hamilton, signer of the Declaration of Independence, co-author of the Federalist Papers explaining the United States Constitution, Secretary of the Treasury under Washington and a founder of the Federalist party.

Hamilton, Jr., was a lawyer, graduate of Columbia College, and a captain of the infantry in the War of 1812.[2] Reduction of the standing army after the war, and the simultaneous national depression found him among those of prestigious ancestry who were in need of work when the Florida territorial government was being organized. U.S. Attorneys got only $200 a year, but it was enough to attract him to Florida for a start. He soon moved into a higher bracket.

He served six months, drew his $100 pay, and was given a more lucrative position as one of three commissioners to settle disputed Spanish land grant claims in East Florida.[3]

His father, the Signer, had left his mother and seven children in debt when he was killed by Aaron Burr in a duel over politics 18 years before, in 1804. Burr and Hamilton, though both Federalists, had long been rivals in New York politics. Burr defeated Hamilton's father-in-law for the U.S. Senate; then he and Thomas Jefferson ran for President in 1800. The electoral college deadlocked. Hamilton threw his support to Jefferson, who was elected, leaving the vice presidency to Burr. In 1804, Burr ran for governor of New York. He lost, with Hamilton opposing him. Hamilton was quoted as saying at a dinner party that he held "a despicable opinion" of Burr. Burr demanded satisfaction in a duel, and fatally shot Hamilton on the same field where Hamilton's eldest son, Philip, was killed in a duel three years earlier. Burr went on to organize a campaign to invade Mexico and set up a new government capital at New Orleans. He was charged with treason, and acquitted—but discredited in many quarters.

It must have been a matter of more than casual concern, then, when Alexander Hamilton, Jr., learned that one of his fellow land claims commissioners at St. Augustine was to be Davis Floyd, who had been charged with treason along with Burr as an active conspirator and captain of one of the boats that carried Burr's expedition down the Ohio and Mississippi rivers. The third commissioner was William A. Blair, who later was named federal judge.[4]

The record doesn't disclose any difficulties between Hamilton and Floyd over the old Burr-Hamilton feud. Hamilton was often a minority of one in disagreements on the land claims board, but most of the division seems to have been over Hamilton's insistence that the other two members weren't as careful about keeping records as they should be. Before they had gone far into the vexatious batch of claims, Hamilton set his political eyes higher.

By an act of Congress approved March 30, 1822, the territory of Florida was entitled to one delegate to Congress, who could speak but not vote. The territorial legislative council called an election for September to name a delegate to serve the last few months of that congressional session. The winner was Joseph M. Hernandez, a Spanish resident of St. Augustine who accepted United States citizenship when Florida was transferred from Spain and was a member of the first territorial legislature. His only opponent for congressional delegate was Dr. James C. Bronough, who died before the election.[5]

In the election for the full term to begin March 3, 1823, Hamilton stepped in as one of four candidates. He only got 249 votes, but that was enough to split the East Florida vote and cause Hernandez to lose the election to Richard Keith Call, then of Pensacola. Call was elected with a plurality 496 to 252 for Hernandez, Hamilton's 249 and 36 for Farquhar Bethune, also of East Florida. It was an East-West division. Call got all but six votes in West Florida, none in East Florida. Hamilton didn't get a single one west of the Suwannee.[6]

There were quick repercussions in St. Augustine. Hamilton was accused of telling Spanish residents their land claims would be jeopardized if they didn't vote for him. Affidavits were filed. Spanish residents petitioned President Monroe to remove Hamilton. They objected that because of his threats "Colonel Alexander Hamilton does not possess those good qualities that ought to adorn a Public Officer."[7] Hamilton denied any such campaign tactics in a letter and affidavits to the President. He said:

> ... If I had been disposed I could have secured my election through two individuals deeply interested in grants. . . . The grantees well know that my integrity is unimpeachable and are imposing upon a few ignorant Minorcans who are in possession of city lots that are unquestionably private property.
>
> I have formed no opinion nor do I entertain any prejudice in hostility to any description of claims.
>
> Permit me to add that this is a most despicable community. I mean the inhabitants of St. Augustine.[8]

Though he should have had better judgment in view of his family record, Hamilton at one point challenged one of his accusers to a duel. It was called off, though, with satisfactory apologies after it was established that the citizen who accused Hamilton of election improprieties didn't know enough English to understand what Hamilton was supposed to have said.[9]

Hamilton doesn't seem to have been happy in St. Augustine. He didn't like the living accommodations, and asked (apparently without success) for permission to occupy a front room in Government House "during the sickly season." He asked that his colleagues on the land claim commission be replaced. When they weren't, he submitted his own resignation March 31, 1824, but changed his mind and tried to withdraw it on May 12.[10] However, it apparently was accepted. He left Florida—and with it the presence of many Burr sympathizers who might be constant reminders of his father's mortal enemy.

Davis Floyd, the old Burr conspirator moved to Tallahassee and became Territorial Treasurer.

Colonel John McKee, Alabama Congressman who was sent to

Tallahassee as Lafayette's land agent, had been an early supporter of Burr's western venture but seems to have pulled out when it began to have treasonable aspects.

Governor William P. Duval had named his eldest son Burr Duval, apparently through some affinity for the discredited former vice president. That would not be surprising. Duval was from Kentucky, and many people along the Ohio and Mississippi river were convinced that Burr was a hero because he only intended to take advantage of an impending Spanish-English war and take over the whole west for the United States.

Favor of such westward expansion was widespread along the Mississippi river. When Lieutenant Edmund P. Gaines arrested Burr in Alabama, he had to take the precaution of disguising him on the trip to Richmond for trial lest aroused symphathizers take him away from the ·troop and free him. Many a child was named for Burr, an enchanting and persuasive man who had a special way with the ladies. That same Lieutenant Edmund P. Gaines became General Gaines, fighting the Indians from Florida to the West. A city in Florida, Gainesville, and a street through the Capitol Center in Talla-hassee are named for him.

There were other Burr shadows moving around in territorial Florida 15 and 20 years after his acquittal for treason.

His only daughter, Theodosia, married Joseph Alston, who became governor of South Carolina. A family of his cousins across the line in Georgia moved from Augusta to Tallahassee and became prominent planters and businessmen. One was killed in a notorious duel, and his brother murdered the killer for revenge.

More closely coincidental, though were the connections of planters in Jefferson county. There was Wirtland, owned by the family of William Wirt, one of Burr's treason trial prosecutors whose summation to the jury was so eloquent school children had to learn and recite it until Lincoln's Gettysburg address replaced it in the text books.[11] And almost next door was Casa Bianca, whose mistress, Florida White, was the daughter of a Kentucky politician who had been so attracted to Burr's venture that it interrupted and threatened to ruin his career.

Alexander Hamilton, Jr., if he was thin skinned at all on the subject might have found too many of the ghosts of his father's nemesis to make him happy if he had stayed much longer in Florida.

NOTES

1. Clarence E. Carter, ed., *The Territorial Papers of the United States*, 27 vols. (Washington, D.C.: United States Government Printing Office, 1956), 22: 413 (hereafter cited as Carter, *Territorial Papers*).

2. Ibid.

3. Ibid., 22:631.

4. Ibid., 22:805.

5. Ibid., 22:528.

6. Ibid., 22:693.

7. Ibid., 22:704.

8. Ibid., 22:708. It is interesting to note that Alexander Hamilton, Jr. used the same word (despicable) in reference to the inhabitants of St. Augustine that his father spoke to provoke the fatal duel with Burr.

9. Hamilton sent his friend Dr. William H. Simmons to John Rodman demanding "satisfaction" for "reflections" on Hamilton's character. Rodman was the Collector of Customs at St. Augustine. A perusal of the Florida Territorial Papers suggests he was also the resident territorial crank. Rodman sent numerous letters to Washington, most of them complaints.

10. Carter, *Territorial Papers*, 22:966.

11. Donald Barr Chidsey, *The Great Conspiracy: Aaron Burr and His Strange Doings in the West* (New York: Crown Publishers Inc., 1967), p. 128.

Chapter Fifteen

Free Among Slaves

Territorial Florida's most direct link with the American revolution may have been through an aged free Negro, Antonio Proctor, who sired one of the state's most respected black families of the 19th century.

"Tony" Proctor, who lived to the age of 112, claimed to have been in Boston when the rebels threw the tea overboard and near Lexington when the "shot heard 'round the world" was fired. His contemporaries believed him. Certainly, he was a guide and aide in trading with the Indians in Spanish Florida; and he became a trusted messenger and interpreter in official American dealings with the Seminoles after the territory was acquired from Spain.

His son, George, was a free and independent building contractor who is credited with erecting some of Tallahassee's finest ante-bellum homes before he joined the California gold rush in 1849. He left the wife he had purchased from slavery with a mortgage note, and a family of children, as security for his debts. He never came back. They were sold for the last five years of slavery, but to friendly white owners who seem to have given them a niche above slaves in general.

John Proctor—grandson of Tony, son of George—became a member of the Florida House of Representatives near the end of the Reconstruction period following the Civil War as a moderate Republican and was elected to the Senate from Leon county four years after white Democrats had wrested the governorship from Republican Carpetbaggers in 1876.

The story of the Proctors has been capably researched and best told in a paper read to the Tallahassee Historical Society in

1943 by Rosalind Parker (Mrs. Russell Collins). Her account, published in the Society's yearbook, Apalachee, for 1946, will be quoted at length here because the original publication is not conveniently available to many readers. She wrote:

Concerning Antonio, Juan de Arredondo y San Felices, Spanish auditor of war, attested in St. Augustine in 1816, "This man is not one of the ordinary mulattoes of the place." Later we find a roster of Florida's prominent men testifying to the same effect. What was said of Antonio could, with equal truth, have been remarked of his son and grandson . . .

Long before the change of flags in 1821, and probably before 1800, Antonio became the property of the Indian trading firm of Panton, Leslie & Co., which employed him as an interpreter. In this capacity, states a memorial of 1848 in his behalf, he acquired "a great knowledge of the Indian character and language and had great influence over the Florida Indians." The Spanish authorities also used him as an interpreter. During the War of 1812, when Florida was attacked by the Patriots and their Indian confederates, Antonio was officially credited with having done "much to pacify the province." In return for his services, Governor José Coppinger in 1816 granted "the free mulatto," Antonio Proctor, 185 acres of land situated in the uncultivated orange grove about five miles from St. Augustine.

How and when Antonio gained his freedom is not known. The Sentinel said he purchased it; the memorial of 1848 said it was for "services faithfully rendered." At any rate, he was a free man in 1816 and probably had been so for many years. He had married about 1798; at the time of Governor Coppinger's grant his family consisted of his wife, a son 17 years old, and four children between the ages of eight and 14. George must have been the youngest or next youngest child, as he was not of age in January, 1829.

The next record we have of Antonio is his purchase, on October 11, 1820, of a lot with a wooden house on St. Francis Street in St. Augustine. Four years later he sold his orange grove.

In the meantime, the change of flags had occurred. Antonio considered himself an American citizen and remained in St. Augustine, true to his new allegiance, during the regime of General Jackson. The position of the Spanish free Negroes was peculiar because the Treaty of Cession stipulated that inhabitants of the ceded provinces should enjoy "all the privileges, rights, and immunities of citizens of the United States." Spanish free Negroes, therefore, always occupied a higher position in Florida than other free Negroes. That may be in part why both Antonio and his son George were at times treated and allowed to do business on exactly the same footing as white men.

Antonio served as an Indian interpreter under the American authorities as he had done during the Spanish regime. In this capacity he was closely associated with Governor William P. Duval, superintendent of Indian affairs for Florida, and Colonel Gad

Humphreys, Indian agent for the territory. It is quite probable that he was present at the Treaty of Camp Moultrie, which was signed on September 24, 1823. Certainly, as shown by records in The National Archives, he was continuously employed as a messenger and interpreter and in carrying presents to the Indians between September 27 and December 30, 1823.

Antonio, or Tony as he is called in later records, continued to act as an interpreter at least until 1834. According to the *Sentinel's* account, he "rendered himself very useful to Genl. Harney and others, as an Indian interpreter in the late Seminole War," but no evidence has been found to substantiate this statement.

"He was much of the largest time at the Seminole agency in East Florida at Fort King." wrote Governor Duval in 1848. . . .
He seems to have been present at the Treaty of Payne's Landing in 1832, for we find him listed as an interpreter in James Gadsden's abstract of expenditures in connection with that treaty. The last time we find him on a payroll is in 1834 at the Apalachicola Agency, which was discontinued about that time.

In endorsing Tony's application to the United States Government for compensation for services between 1824 and 1827 for which he claimed never to have been paid, Governor Duval in 1848 gave his estimate of the old Negro's character and services. "Tony Proctor is well known to me as a man of truth and integrity . . ." wrote Duval. "The Indians were scattered over Florida and Proctor was often required to summon the chiefs to meet me on business at Tallahassee, or to meet the Indian agent at Fort King . . . Proctor was of great service in controling the Indians and rendered me, and the country, most essential benefits, from his usefulness with the Indians and his prudence and good sense—no man could have possessed there confidence in a higher degree . . . his services were invaluable to the United States—in the management of the Florida Indians at a period when no other person could have preserved the peace of the country."

Tony Proctor's connnection with Tallahassee began the summer the town was founded. In a statement of payments made to him in 1824 and 1825 is the following: "July 21, 1824 as express in bringing letters to Tallahassee 31.50." During the next few years Tony's duties must have made him a frequent visitor to the new capital. . . .[1]

Tony was well paid for his services. Official territorial papers reveal he received $672.68, all told, between November 14, 1823 and December 1, 1824—scarcely over a year—for taking presents to the Indians, carrying letters between agencies of government, standing as interpreter in dealing with the Seminoles and conducting them to land assigned to them by treaty.[2] That was good money for the time—more than a third the Governor's annual salary, and three times the pay of a United States Attorney.

The esteem which Antonio Proctor was held is indicated by
the fact that his obituary ran almost a full column in the
Florida Sentinel of July 3, 1855. It is the only known obituary
for a Negro to have been published in a Tallahassee newspaper
prior to the end of the Civil War; and it received space
commensurate with that given to death notices of only the most
prominent white citizens. The *Sentinel* carried this report under
a simple headline, "A Natural Death"—

Died at the residence of H. L. Rutgers Esq. of this City on
Saturday the 10th ult. of old age, Toney Proctor, a free man of color
in his 112th year— "Uncle Toney," as he was familiarly called must
have been at the time of his death at least 112 years of age and the
probabilities are that he was several years older. It is known as a
historical fact that he was at the battle of Quebec, on the 13th of
Sept. 1759 some 95 years ago. His recollection of that event was
clear and distinct. He was there in the capacity of a body servant to
an English officer, and was sixteen years of age, or more at the time
of sailing in company with the English soldier, from the Island of
Jamaica to return no more to the place of his nativity. He was
subsequently engaged in the same capacity, though under a different
officer, during the early period of the Revolutionary war, between
this and the mother country. He was at the vicinity of Boston at the
time the tea was thrown overboard, and afterwards at the battle of
Lexington, where the first blood was spilt in that perilous conflict.
Just here there is another wide gap in his history, which we are
unable to trace— It is known, however, that he came to Florida long
before the change of flags, and settled in St. Augustine, where he
purchased his freedom, married and reared a large family. During his
long residence in the "Ancient City," where he experienced many
reverses—living through a period usually allotted to an ordinary life
time, his conduct was such as to command the esteem and respect of
its inhabitants, as well under the administration of the United States,
as the dominion of Spain.

At the change of flags, he considered himself an American citizen,
and remained in St. Augustine true to his allegiance during the
campaigns and military regime of General Jackson; and subsequently
rendered himself very useful to General Harney and others, as an
Indian interpreter in the late Seminole War.

Coming out of that protracted and disastrous war reduced in
circumstances, with nothing to rely upon for support, except a claim
upon the Government for services rendered, but little of which was
ever recognized and paid, he came some ten years or more to
Tallahassee to live with his son George.

In 1849, George went a gold hunting, with the intention, if
successful, to return in a few years at furtherest and relieve himself
of his embarrassments. In the mean time, his family, as well as
"Uncle Toney," were left in charge of Mr. Rutgers. They have been
well cared for during his absence, Mr. R. often advancing supplies for
their support, upon the faith of remittances from California, but

neither George nor the remittances in all cases have been forth-
coming. But it was not so much our purpose to attempt to trace his
traditionary story, as briefly to notice the peculiar circumstances of
his death. We have deemed it not out of place, however to preface it
with a brief sketch of his life span cut through an extraordinary
period of time, the events and visiscitudes of which were, to say the
least of them, very remarkable for one of his race.—Had he been an
educated man with the blood of the Anglo Saxons flowing in his
veins, he could not have failed, passing through the same stirring
scenes, to have left his mark on the history of [Florida. And as it
was] may be said of him, in consideration of his long residence in
Florida, and the part he acted in her history, that he was a man who
in the course of his career, "rendered some service to the State."

The circumstance attending his death, were very remarkable. He
died of no disease. His health continued good and his spirits cheerful
down to within a day or so of his death. The first evidence of decay
was that of sight; time in other respects working but little change in
his appearance. This organ had almost entirely failed him. His
memory too, was most singularly affected. He apparently had lucid
intervals. At times his recollection of the past, was clear and distinct,
and then again, his memory seemed to have completely deserted
him. Connected with this evidence of mental decay, is this peculiar
circumstance. His memory or idea of locality never failed him,
though he forgot his friends, except those with whom he was in
daily intercourse. His locomotion also continued good. If his meals
were not sent to him regularly, he would go after them, walking
from his cabin to the house, a distance of more than one hundred
yards. This he did the day before his death. He usually ate heartily,
and his appetite continued good to the last. He complained of no
pains—no sickness, no aches of any kind. Being asked on Saturday
morning how he felt, replied, "Ah Ben I'm going." His extremities
felt cold and his breathing began to grow short, until he breathed no
more.— Death seem to come upon him like falling into a gentle
sleep, literally burned out. Uncle Toney was much beloved by his
own people. A zealous member of the Baptist Church, his funeral on
Sunday afternoon, was one of the largest processions we remember
to have witnessed.

Though all evidence indicates Antonio Proctor was in the
service of a British officer, if he took part in the American
revolution at all, no doubt has been raised about his loyalty and
devotion to the United States from the time Florida was taken
over from Spain.

Life was not easy for a free Negro during slave times and
Antonio's son, George, had problems from boyhood which had
him often in court. Lee Warner, director of research for the
Tallahassee Historic Preservation Board, offers the opinion that
George Proctor would have been as great a success as anyone in
early Tallahassee except for one circumstance—he couldn't

declare bankruptcy, as others did during periods of economic distress, because it would have meant having his family sold, and perhaps even himself, into slavery in distribution of his assets among creditors.

Nevertheless George held his own in service and competition with the white tradesmen of early Tallahassee.

He came of age and started his career as an independent business operator about 1830. The Parker paper offered details:

His first business transaction of which we have record was the purchase of a town lot for $30 on October 17, 1831. The previous year, Tony had bought two town lots, which he later sold to his son. The records of transactions by the Proctors show that the son could sign his name but the father had to make his mark. A single specimen of George's signature is extant. Its unformed and practically undecipherable character suggests that his ability to write was limited to the two words of his name.

George was a carpenter by trade, and a good one. In a few years he was virtually a contractor. He built at least eight houses in Tallahassee that are still standing today (1943). . . .[3]

During these years George was investing small sums in real estate and selling at a profit. In 1833 he bought two lots at a city tax sale for $1.06¼ and $1.25 which he later sold for $50 and $65. In 1834 he paid $60 for a lot which he sold the next year for $405. In October, 1836, he paid $350 for lot 101 in the North Addition; in March, 1838, he sold it to R. B. Copeland for $3,510. The only reasonable explanation of this transaction is that he built a house on the lot before selling to Mr. Copeland.

All available evidence indicates that George did business on equal terms with white men. This may have been due to his status as a Spanish free Negro, whose rights were guaranteed under the Treaty of 1819; it also may have been attributable to the exceptional character of the man. At any rate, in 1839 he was paying a white poll tax rather than the higher poll tax levied on free Negroes. In that year his property was assessed at $1,500.

Affairs were going well for George in the late Thirties and he assumed heavier and heavier obligations. On April 2, 1838, he contracted with Henry Bond to buy lots 1 and 2 on the original plan of the city, giving two notes for $500 payable on January 1, 1839, and January 1, 1840. The next year he decided to settle down and get married. This was a fateful decision in a fateful period after the Panic of 1837, for the woman he wished to marry was a slave.

On May 8, 1839, George Proctor was married in St. John's Episcopal Church to Nancy Chandler by the Reverend Francis P. Lee, The record reads, "a free black who purchased his wife." This transaction finally ruined George.

Nancy was the property of Mrs. Mary Chandler, who then ran a boarding house in Tallahassee and was originally from the Eastern Shore of Maryland. The price agreed on was $1,300, not exorbitant for a good slave who was probably a trained house servant. George paid $450 in cash and agreed to pay the remaining $850, with interest at an unspecified rate, in one year's time. As securities for his debt he gave Mrs. Chandler both his personal note for $850 and a mortgage on Nancy. Two white men, Alexander Formy Duval and Louis Demilly, went on his note.

The year passed and George was unable to meet his note. The after effects of the Panic of 1837 were beginning to be seriously felt in Tallahassee and times were hard. George could neither meet his own obligations nor collect money owing to him. He soon found himself in the center of a maze of lawsuits, the most important of which were filed by Mrs. Chandler.

On October 26, 1840, Thompson & Hagner, attorneys for Mrs. Chandler, sued George in Leon Superior Court for $1,700 on his $850 note. The plaintiff alleged that in addition to the amount of the note, the defendant was further indebted to her on October 1, 1840, in the sum of $900. A possible explanation of this statement is the fact that Nancy either had given, or was about to give, birth to a child, who would become the property of the mother's owner. On February 13, 1841, Mrs. Chandler entered suit for foreclosure of the mortgage on Nancy.

The two cases were determined in December, 1841. A jury awarded Mrs. Chandler $1,023 on the note, being the principal and interest compounded semiannually at 10 per cent, but disregarded the claim for the additional $900. Judge Samuel J. Douglas then entered a decree in the foreclosure suit giving George until March 1, 1842, to pay the judgment. If it was not paid by that date, an execution was to be issued for a levy on Nancy and any other property that George might have.

On January 24, 1842, Mrs. Chandler filed her affidavit stating that she had "good reason to believe" that George would remove Nancy from the Territory of Florida before the execution could be levied upon. Judge Douglas thereupon ordered that execution be issued immediately. What happened next we do not know. We can only assume that some white friend, possibly Henry L. Rutgers, paid Mrs. Chandler and had the judgment assigned to himself. Certainly Nancy was not levied upon at this time. The judgment, however, was left hanging over George.

His other creditors were pressing him. His multitudinous debts included $186.16 to William H. Francis, tin merchant; $321 to Francis H. Flagg; $1,038.20 to Thomas and Richard Haywood, merchants; $160.50 to Robert H. Berry and James Dowling, merchants; $240.98 to Jesse Atkinson; and, with William Weedon, another free Negro, $181.47 to the estate of E. B. Vass. How he satisfied most of these claims cannot be ascertained. Some of his real estate was levied upon in 1846 to satisfy judgments in favor of Atkinson and Vass; one lot was also levied upon to satisfy in very small part the Chandler judgment. But George must have managed to meet his other obligations in some way.

By this time the Proctor family consisted of Nancy, the wife; Florida, a daughter baptised at home in 1840 by the Episcopal minister; Charlotte, Georgianna, and a fourth child, John Proctor,

born in a house at the corner of Adams and Call Streets, January 14,
1844, the year before Florida became a state. These children were
baptised September 15, 1844, by the Reverend William H. C.
Yeager. Later on, Machaimum Stewart, Mary Magalene, and George,
Jr., were baptised March 4, 1849. Apparently there was an eighth
child, Bahamia, for whom there is no baptismal record. According to
John Proctor, George persuaded his cousin, Lydia Stout, to come
from the Bahamas to be a governess for his children.

During the Forties George continued to ply his trade as a
carpenter. Work seems to have been slack, however, and he is said to
have gone to St. Marks at one time to work on a wharf. In 1846 he
tried farming, renting land and hiring Negroes from Benjamin F.
Allen. The venture was unsuccessful, and in July, 1848, he was
forced to give Allen a crop and chattel lien to secure a debt of
$450. . . .[4]

Word that gold was found in California offered George
Proctor a chance to get out from under his debts.

A party of Tallahasseeans of equally distressed or adventure-
some circumstances was making up for a trek to the gold fields.

A notice in the *Floridian* of January 6, 1849 said:

> For California! The undersigned propose to leave for California
> between this time and the first of March next, and would be pleased
> to be accompanied by such of their fellow citizens as may desire to
> seek their fortunes in this new land of promise. Their route of travel
> will be left to be determined by themselves and their companions
> when the expedition is fully organized.
>
> All persons wishing to join the party must be of healthy
> constitutions—must possess at least three hundred dollars in money
> and come to them well recommended as to moral character. Thomas
> Hayward, Sen'r., W. M. Maxwell, W. Bartlett, O. S. Burroughs, Geo.
> O. McMullin, W. N. Taylor, Richard B. Maxwell.

George Proctor apparently joined the party. The *Floridian*
and *Journal* for March 10, 1849, has this item:

> Card—In bidding adieu to my friends and patrons, I would return
> them my most sincere thanks and heartfelt gratitude for the
> kindness, liberality and patronage extended to me from the days of
> my boyhood to the present. George Proctor.

The next, and final, direct word we have of George Proctor
comes from the obituary column of the San Francisco,
California, *Elevator*, of January 15, 1869—nearly 20 years after
he left Tallahassee:

DIED

In Sonora, Tuolumne County, December 26, 1868, George
Proctor, a native of Florida, aged 63 years, 8 months and 3 days.
(Florida papers please copy.)

Mr. Proctor was an old resident of Sonora, where he has lived since 1850, and was highly respected by all who knew him. A gentleman of Sonora who knew him well, writes us as follows:

He was a native of Florida, was born a free man; at an early age he married a slave, by whom he had three or four children; before coming to California he purchased the freedom of his wife and children and left the papers with a lawyer in whom he had the utmost confidence, until he should come to California and make money enough and send for them. In the meantime, his friend, the lawyer, became involved and betrayed the trust of Proctor, and sold his wife and children. Proctor wrote repeatedly to his old home but never got an answer; and finally gave it up—hence his zeal in the cause of freedom for his color."

The Florida version is not quite so damning of George Proctor's treatment in Tallahassee. The Parker paper reviews it:

In California, instead of seeking gold, George went on with contracting and building. Work was plentiful and he made twelve dollars a day. He tried to write to his family, but according to hearsay, Nancy was allowed to receive only one letter, which she was forced to surrender. He is said to have sent back some gold nuggets, but not enough to change the status of his family. . . .

After 1847, Florida law required each free Negro to have a guardian. According to local tradition, Dr. Call first served as guardian of George Proctor and his slave family; later Argyle and Bond, the commission merchants, acted in that capacity, and lastly Henry L. Rutgers. Certainly, the family was under the care of Rutgers after George went to California.

John Proctor was nine when he and his family were sold to Jane Rutgers for $2,300 on February 6, 1854. The sale, by Haley T. Blocker, sheriff, was made to satisfy the judgment in favor of Mrs. Chandler, which had been hanging over the family for twelve years. The seven Negroes named in the bill of sale were Nancy, Charlotte, Georgianna, John, Bahamia, Mary, and George. Presumably, Florida and Machaimum Stewart had died in infancy. . . .

Mr. and Mrs. Rutgers soon found it necessary to use the Proctor slaves as security for obligations resulting from transactions with the Union Bank. Indeed, assuming that the Chandler judgment had been assigned to Mr. Rutgers in 1842, it is quite likely that execution of the judgment in 1854 had been necessitated by his own financial difficulties. A $3,000 mortgage in favor of the Union Bank, placed on the Proctors in 1858, was satisfied the following year by John L. Rutgers, of New York, but in January, 1860, Charlotte, Mary, and George were sold to Colonel George W. Scott for $2,800. Until slave days were over, the other children were hired out. Georgianna worked for Mr. Fernando and later for Mr. B. C. Lewis; John and Bahamia were hired to Mr. Robert Williams. . . .[5]

John Proctor became a special sort of slave in ante-bellum Tallahassee—bound by law, but apparently helped and encouraged to receive some education while slaves in general were

being denied the opportunity lest they rebel, escape and join
the gathering abolition movement. Miss Parker, who got some
of her information from Proctor himself before he died
December 15, 1944, a month prior to his 101st birthday,
reports he was taught to read and write by Willy Ames, the
railroad depot agent, and to work arithmetic by Banker B. C.
Lewis.

"When freedom came, John was prepared for it," she wrote.

As a member of the Republican party, John was qualified for
political jobs. At one time he was appointed one of nine commissioners to inspect the coaling station at Key West. He did not get
the money promised him because Colonel Malachi Martin, the
paymaster, and a Mr. Craig beat the commissioners out of it.
Luckily, though, John had a real friend in Mr. B. C. Lewis, who
warned him ahead of time to withdraw his money from the ill-fated
Freedman's Bank.

For several years John taught plantation schools: two terms at
Polly Chaires, ten miles from Tallahassee; two terms on the Parkhill
plantation at Tuscawilla; and finally two terms at Long Pond, fifteen
miles from Tallahassee. None of these schools had more than five
months in the term and the pay was small—less than forty dollars a
month. John also served as a mail clerk under the one-armed Negro
postmaster, William G. Steward.

In 1869 John Proctor was married to Mary Mason by the
Reverend James Smith, pastor of the Tallahassee Colored Methodist
Episcopal Church. . . .

All the while politics were becoming more and more interesting.
John had run unsuccessfully for the House of Representatives in
1870. In 1872 he stumped Leon County with his white friend, Dr.
Simon B. Conover, of New Jersey, in opposition to candidates of the
Osborn-Purman Ring. Both Proctor and Conover were elected, as
was John Wallace. Wallace and Proctor were two of five men who
refused to attend the 1873 Republican caucus of House members.
The five recalcitrant Republicans combined with the full Democratic
strength of the House to elect Dr. Conover speaker over the Ring
candidate, John R. Scott, Negro representative from Duval County.

The vote had been 28 for Conover to 20 for Scott. This presaged
defeat for the Ring candidate for United States senator unless
something could be done to change the alignment of votes. The Ring
strategy was to unseat enough legally elected Democrats to give the
Ring a majority. But John Wallace, whom Conover had appointed
chairman of the important Committee on Privileges and Elections,
was pledged not to unseat any member who had been honestly
elected. The Osborn faction sought to reach Wallace through
Proctor. Wallace relates that one of the Osborn managers gave John
$700 "to be used to influence the chairman to report in favor of the
[Republican] contestants. Proctor took the money and bought two
mules for his farm and requested the chairman to stand his
ground.". . . .

All efforts to corrupt Wallace, Proctor, and the other anti-Ring Republicans failed. Dr. Conover, the anti-Ring candidate, was elected United States senator.

As John had been elected for a two-year term in 1872, he served in the session of 1874. He was reelected in that year as a member of the 1875 session. He acted as a supervisor of elections for Leon County precinct No. 3 in 1876. Defeated for the House in 1876, he was elected again in 1878 and served in the 1879 session. He was defeated again in 1880, but in 1882 he was elected senator from Leon County and, as such, sat in the Legislatures of 1883 and 1885. He was the home senator for Governor William D. Bloxham, with whom he got along very well. . . .

Throughout, John Proctor was a moderate Republican. The one thing he was proud of during his long life was that there was no serious trouble between the Negroes and the whites in Leon County. There was plenty of inflammable material, for Leon was a black-belt county. It took wise leadership from both white and colored men to prevent trouble.

John's last political position as superintendent of customs at St. Marks was probably the best of his career. Doing business on the side, he kept a fish and oyster house and ran a freight and passenger transportation service.

When white supremacy was re-established. John adjusted himself to the changed conditions and found work as a brick mason.

He returned to the Episcopal church, in which he had been christened, and for years was a communicant of St. John's Church. . . .[6]

John Proctor's respectability among his white contemporaries never died.

The author recalls a conversation about him with Justice J. B. Whitfield of the State Supreme Court when Proctor was nearing his 100th birthday. Though Judge Whitfield was some years younger, they had shared some political experiences (Whitfield had covered the 1885 constitutional convention for Jacksonville and Savannah newspapers). He was open in his esteem and fondness for the aged Negro. "I don't see him often," the judge said. "He got too old to come and see me; so now I go to see him." But the judge's age and work were making the visits less and less frequent, he lamented. It was a relationship between white and black men which was less strange in the South of that period than many legends would have us believe.

Surely, there was a family—Antonio, George and John Proctor—which in three generations would have been ranked foremost among the pioneers of Florida except for one factor it could not control—color of skin.

NOTES

1. Rosalind Parker, "The Proctors—Antonio, George, and John," *Apalachee* (1946): 19-21 (hereafter cited as Parker, "The Proctors").

2. Clarence E. Carter, ed., *The Territorial Papers of the United States,* 27 vols. (Washington, D.C.: United States Government Printing Office, 1956), 22:141-144.

3. Two houses identifiable as the work of George Proctor still standing in 1976 are the Randall House on the southwest corner of Calhoun and Carolina streets and the Garden Center house at 507 North Calhoun Street. He also has been credited with three six-room houses on the south side of East Park avenue between Calhoun and Gadsden streets. Parker, "The Proctors", p. 22.

4. Ibid., pp. 21-25.

5. Ibid., pp. 25-26.

6. Ibid., pp. 27-28. For further information on Reconstruction in Florida see W. T. Cash, *The Story of Florida* (New York: The American Historical Society, 1938), William W. Davis, *The Civil War and Reconstruction in Florida* (Gainesville: University of Florida Press, 1964), and Jerrell H. Shofner, *Nor Is It Over Yet* (Gainesville: University Presses of Florida, 1974).

Postscript

If these capsules of Florida history satisfy the casual readers, the authors and publishers will feel rewarded.

If, however, they only whet the desire of scholars to dig deeper than the sources we have exploited, our gratification will increase as the volume of historical lore grows. We will delight in having helped start a continuing contribution, in this national bicentennial year, to the history of Florida; for we feel that a citizenry which pays no attention to its past can't really fulfill its future.

We have had to omit from these essays much that is known about some of the characters. We have found gaps and discrepancies in the facts and commentaries about others which need to be filled to complete the picture of our heritage.

There is one more chapter in this book. It doesn't comport with the general theme of Floridians who had some family connection with the Revolutionary period; but it describes Tallahassee as it was found by the capital's first newspaperman. We justify its inclusion here because we have found it, we don't know of any previous republication in a book of general circulation, and we believe it will be of interest.

The First Dateline

Tallahassee's first newspaper, the *Florida Intelligencer*, was established by Ambrose Crane on February 19, 1825, less than three months after the first legislature convened in the new capital and nine months before the town was incorporated.

What probably is the first Tallahassee dateline to appear in the national press is found in the *National Intelligencer* of Washington. On April 9, 1825, it published this report under the headline: "TALLAHASSEE—In Florida."

> We received, yesterday, the first number of a new paper, printed in Florida, at Tallahassee, the spot fixed upon and recently occupied as the Seat of Government, by the title of the "Florida Intelligencer." The following account of this "young capital" will be interesting to most of our readers, some of whom have scarcely ever heard the name of it:

> TALLAHASSEE—This young capital of Florida is already attracting the attention of capitalists. Many buildings are erecting, and others are in a state of preparation, even before the sale of the lots, which will take place on the fourth day of April next. It is situated on a beautiful and commanding eminence, about 18 miles north of St. Marks, in the bosom of a fertile and picturesque country. The south side of the town is watered by innumerable springs of pure water, and a clear and pleasant stream passes by the east and south sides, at the distance of a few yards, and after passing the town as if sensible the point of its usefulness was past, falls over the rock which beds the stream, forming a pleasant cascade, and passes off by a subterraneous passage.[1]

> The country around Tallahassee, and extending from the Suwannee to near the Apalachicola river, has deservedly attracted the attention of travellers, and those who have visited it with a view of a

permanent settlement. The fertile lands between the above mentioned rivers extend from east to west from eighty to one hundred miles, and from north to south about fifteen miles. This tract of country, much of which is adapted to the culture of sugar,[2] is finely watered by the tributary streams of the Suwannee, the St. Marks, Wakulla, Okelockoney, Little river and several other smaller rivers and streams, and is beautifully studded with lakes and ponds of the purest water. The land is rolling, with here and there an eminence, that rises considerably above the surrounding country, which will afford delightful seats for the opulent men of leisure.

This country, notwithstanding its singular beauty and fertility, becomes more interesting from the indubitable evidence of its having been once densely populated by a civilized race of men. Almost every eminence is capped with ancient fortifications, which appear regular, and some of them substantially formed. At Fort St. Lewis,[3] about two miles west of Tallahassee, have been found remnants of iron cannon, spikes, hinges, locks, etc. which are evidently of Spanish manufacture, and which have not been much injured by the rust.

Within the principal fort, for the outworks seem to have been numerous and extensive, are the ruins of two brick edifices; one was about sixty feet by forty, the other about thirty by twenty. These are in total ruins, and nothing but a mound appears where the walls stood, composed wholly of broken bricks, which had been composed of a coarse sandy clay, and burned in the modern fashion. Yet on the very walls of these buildings, are oaks, eighteen inches in diameter. On the same hill, and in fact within the outworks of this fort, are to be seen grape arbors in parallel lines, which still maintain their pristine regularity.

Bricks seem to have been in general use, for they have been discovered in several places by digging a little below the surface of the earth. Within the town of Tallahassee some were dug up, having a substance adhering to them resembling lime morter. But on the hill, about a half a mile south-east of the Capitol, are to be seen the greatest proof of a dense population. On this hill are to be seen streets or roads, running nearly at right angles, at such distances as demonstrate the former existence of a pretty large town. The shade trees of the former inhabitants still remain, and are generally of live oak, and near which may be discovered grape arbors of more or less regularity. In several instances we discovered a species of the plumb tree.

There has been much speculation and inquiry concerning the former inhabitants of this country, who they were, and at what time they flourished. No records are within our reach, and the Spanish inhabitants at the extremes of the Territory had no knowledge of this country, much less of the people, who once lived here, but have

long since disappeared.[4] Some, however, say that records of the fact
do exist at Havanna, and that measures have been taken to obtain
them—that Leon was the adventurer, who led a colony hither, but
the precious metals of South America and Mexico so occupied the
attention of the Spanish Government, that this infant colony was
suffered to fall a prey to the Indians.

The traditionary accounts of the Indians are very plausible, and
are corroborated by many existing and circumstantial facts. They
claimed this country at their late treaty at St. Augustine as belonging
to them by right of conquest, achieved by their ancestors. They
represent, that it was once densely populated by a race of white
men, who settled in this country, and incorporated themselves with
the Yamassee Indians. — That the Yamassees adopted their habits
and became Christians, but ceased to be fighting men. That this
people had fine houses, carriages, herds of cattle, etc. and made wide
roads, and bridges over rivers and streams of water. That they also
had many forts and big guns. At this time the Creek Indians made
frequent attacks upon them, but were generally unsuccessful, as they
then fought with bows and spears only, for they had not yet learned
the use of the rifle. At length, after losing many warriors, they
associated with themselves all the tribes between Georgia and the
Mississippi, with many others far in the North, and came down
unexpectedly into this country. The white inhabitants generally fled
to their forts, while most of the Yamassees fell into their hands.
Then men were put to death, but the women and children were
carried into captivity.[5]

They carried universal desolation over the face of the country, as
the surest method of reducing the fortified places. They had made
many attempts to storm these, and bound thick pieces of wood
before their persons, as a protection from the bullets, but the big
guns broke their defences in pieces, and destroyed their warriors. At
length famine and war destroyed all save the garrison in Fort St.
Louis. This, after resisting every diversity of attack, was at last
abandoned and destroyed, and the garrison retired to a considerable
fort near the mouth of the Okelockony, where was afterwards
fought a great and decisive battle, which made the Creeks masters of
the country.

The Indians designed, when they undertook to possess themselves
of the country, to settle and reside here. But, as they expressed it,
they were too foolish and had rendered it uninhabitable. They had
destroyed the houses, and there was no wood to build others. They
had destroyed or consumed the domestic animals, and there was no
game to subsist them. They were, therefore, obliged to retire from
the scenes of their own desolation, a small part west of the
Apalachicola river, and the others of their own country.[6]

Many of the leading statements in the foregoing account are strongly corroborated by circumstances and facts within the knowledge of many Americans. This is said to be the country of the ancient Yamassees, and it is a fact that the Creeks have held a slave race, descended from the Yamassee nation, which has but recently been incorporated with their tribe. It is also a fact, that forts were very numerous, and that Fort St. Louis bears evident marks of having been destroyed by the whites from the mutilated appearance of the cannon, which must have been broken by sledge hammers.[7] There is also said to be a very considerable fortification in the neighbourhood of the Okelockony. From the growth of the forest trees, it must have been about two hundred years since the country was laid waste. Be that as it may, it is rapidly populating anew, and the power of the natives is now broken. We have nothing to fear from them, and they cannot, if they would, repeat the desolating scenes which once swept over this beautiful domain.—*Fl. Intell.*

NOTES

1. The scene described is in the area recently rescued from slum conditions for recreation of a Cascades Park on the southeast perimeter of the Capitol Center.

2. Several early planters, notably Thomas Brown, made the mistake of trying to produce sugar cane in the Tallahassee area. The first harsh weather destroyed the vision. Governor Thomas A. Brown, 1863, "Memoirs," unpublished manuscript, Tallahassee, Florida.

3. Fort San Luis, destroyed in Moore's raid of 1704.

4. They were the Apalachees. See Chapter 1.

5. A fairly accurate account of what happened, but with no information on the British participation.

6. This picture of desolation most likely is apocryphal. It does not stand to reason that a force of a thousand men could utterly destroy the forest and game of Apalachee in 1704 or even today.

7. The Spanish destroyed their own Fort San Luis to keep it from falling into the hands of Moore, who had burned neighboring missions.

Acknowledgements

Hardly any book is a one-man work. This one certainly isn't. We are grateful for help from many quarters.

Louise Jordan has brought order to haphazard scraps of manuscript coming in sparetime spurts, evening out their flow to the printer (as she has done for so many years for the editorial pages of the *Tallahassee Democrat*).

Authors of papers published over the years by the Tallahassee Historical Society in its yearbook, Apalachee, have contributed much. So have the facsimile reproductions of historic Florida books by the University Presses of Florida.

Members of the Florida State Library and the Florida State University library staff have been helpful.

Special thanks goes to Randolph Whitfield of Atlanta, Dr. John Chipman of Cambridge, Massachusetts, and to Rev. Joseph John Jones of Chesapeake, Virginia, for help on the Eppes-Randolph Chapter; to Mrs. Carter Smith of the Mobile Historic Preservation Society for contributions to the Walton Chapter; Miles Womack, Quincy historian and Charlie Dickey for information about Patrick Henry's grandson; J. Lewis Hall, Sr., for looking up ancient Masonic records, Dr. James Reddick for data on Florida White and Dr. Dorothy Dodd, retired State Librarian for data supplied over many years which made this task easier.

For help in rounding up and preparing illustrations we are indebted to Claribel Jett, Tallahassee portraitist who let us use her work; to Joan Morris of the FSU Library photographic archives; to Nancy Dobson and Lee Warner of the Tallahassee Historic Preservation Board; to our daughter Donna Moorer; to

Fred W. Metzke who designed the jacket; and to photographers and artists of the Tallahassee Democrat—Sage Thigpen, Earl Warren, Ray Stanyard, Dan Stainer, Dave Wallace and Carol Kreider.

Many others have helped but the whole project would not have been undertaken except for the volunteer personal donations by these Rotarians of enough money to pay all the research and other pre-publication expenses:

ROTARY CLUB OF TALLAHASSEE

William L. Adams, Jr.
James M. Alford
Sydney D. Andrews
John K. Arnold
Philip F. Ashler
David A. Avant, Jr.
George D. Avant
P. Peter Ballas
John W. Barr
Pearce L. Barrett, Jr.
Charles Barrier
Jon S. Beazley*
Ben F. Betts, Jr.
Garth K. Blake
Luke H. Blanton, Jr.
Al B. Block
Hyman H. Bluestein
James O. Boman
Ruel L. Bradley, Jr.
John D. Bridges
Francis R. Bridges, Jr.
Robert T. Brinkley*
Richard N. Brock
J. Rae Brown
Norborne A. Brown, Jr.
Walter F. Buchan
Clifford E. Campbell
Paul J. Cannedy
F. Wilson Carraway, Jr.
Marshall R. Cassedy
John E. Champion
Judson M. Chapman
Mrs. J. V. Chapman
W. Judd Chapman
T. Edwin Chason
Thad J. Chason
Dean A. Chenoweth, Sr.
Robert I. Clark
Merritt R. Clements
Fred Wayne Cook
C. Huxley Coulter, Sr.
Clinton H. Coulter, Jr.
Edwin D. Crane III
Robert C. Crooks
Walter V. Culley II
Jack M. Culpepper
Dorrance F. Dalrymple
Robert C. Daniel
L. Saxon Dasher
Ernest S. Doster
J. Hamilton Dowling, Jr.
William I. DuBey

Wilton Duncan, Jr.
Clark Durrance
William Dyer
Merton L. Ekwall
Lee W. Elgin, Jr.
Colin English, Jr. President
Colin English, Sr.
Homer S. Fisher
Robert Chester Francis
William W. Francis
Walter G. Frauenheim, Jr.
Elmer O. Friday
Ralph Gallington
Michael J. Gonatos
William Graham
Ray E. Green, Sr.
Marshall Hamilton
Samuel E. Hand*
Sam Hand, Jr.
Emmett C. Harrison
I. Barnett Harrison*
Walter H. Harwell, Jr.*
C. D. Hasbrouck
Frank W. Hazelton
Edward B. Henderson
Gordon B. Henkel
Charles W. Hill
H. Louis Hill
Patrick W. Hogan
William C. Holley
Wiley L. Housewright*
Joe R. Hughes
Richard E. Hulet
Paul Hunt
A. C. Johnson
Malcolm B. Johnson*
Tom C. Johnson
Cale R. Keller
Henry Jervey Kelly
Clarence W. Ketchum
Daniel A. Kleman
Nelson H. Kraeft
M. A. LaBorde
Angus McK. Laird
George E. Lambert
Charles Lamm
Carroll G. Lance
Jay Landers
Ronnie L. Leavel
Robert E. Lee
Ryals E. Lee
William S. Lee

George Edward Lewis II
Thomas B. Lipe
Robert G. Maige
Hank Mannheimer
John M. Marr
Stanley Marshall
Burrel J. Mawhinney
Stephen D. McClellan
J. Robert McClure, Jr.
David C. McNamara
Patrick H. Mears
Robert V. Mears
Fred W. Metzke*
Stephen Metzke
Payne H. Midyette, Jr.
Miley L. Miers, Jr.
Harold K. Mikell
Samuel Edward Miller
E. R. Mills
J. W. Mitchell
Peter B. Mitchell, Jr.
Frank D. Moor
Sam H. Moorer, Jr.
Sam J. Myers
F. Joseph Nahoom
Stephen O'Connell
Hoke S. Oliver
William J. Oven, Jr.*
Ben F. Overton
Robert C. Parker
Robert Parker, Jr.*
Leonard W. Parkhurst
Robert D. Peacock
J. K. Peddie
William Peterson
James R. Pope
Melvin L. Pope, Jr.
Broward Poppell
Ralph Edward Proctor, Jr.
W. Theo Proctor, Jr.
W. Theo Proctor, Sr.
William F. Rehbaum III
Francis A. Rhodes*
Raymond E. Rhodes
Earl Rhody
Robert A. Riedel
E. Grover Rivers
Dixon Galt Robinson
Jack A. Robinson
Samuel B. Rogers
Charles A. Rovetta
Allen Sapp

Edward J. Sessions
Robert E. Shackleton
James S. Shaw
Stanley A. Sheppard
Albert B. Sherrill*
William F. Shipman
Robert M. Shoemaker
John A. Simpson
George Slager
H. Lawrence Smith, Jr.
John Orson Smith, Jr.
Roger C. Smith
Richard Ernest Snow

Ben Sowell
William H. Stafford
Albert H. Stephens
Louis B. St. Petery, Jr.
J. Ed Straughn
James E. Swain
Sam C. Tatum
Ray C. Tindall
Joseph B. Tinker
Arthur C. Tonkinson
Ramsey R. Trimble
C. Ben Tucker, Jr.
Fred W. Turner

Paul R. Turner
Ben F. Waddill
Thomas A. Waits
J. Edwin White
John W. White
John T. Wigginton
Klein Wigginton
H. Corter Williams
J. T. Williams, Jr.
Thomas Lynn Wollschlager
Thomas P. Wood
J. Howard Woodward
William E. Woodward
William F. Woodward

NORTHSIDE ROTARY CLUB

Earl Bacon
Cecil Beach
Homer Brinkley
Emory Cain, President
Orlis Causseaux
George Clarke
Robert F. Coyne
David E. Craig
Joe Culley II
Robert C. Davidge
Sam Davidson
Jerry Deloney
Lawrence Evans
Eugene Figg, Jr.
Robert Fincher
Richard Gardner, Jr.
Stanley Garfein
A. T. Gibson, Jr.
Charles K. Hill*
Hubert Hunt

Richard Ingram
Norman James
J. L. Larkin
Ed Liedy
William Lindsey
Owen Mahan
James Maples, Jr.
Glenn McClane
Harold McVey
Harold Mendelson
Sidney Mendelson
David Miles
Joshua Morse III
John Mowell
Gerald Murphy
Robert O'Connell
William M. Phillips
Don Pumphrey
Bryan Robinson*
Charles Rockwood

Charles E. Salter
Joe Samere
Vernon Sanders
William C. Smith*
Daniel Snead
T. Q. Srygley*
Errol Stafford
John Swartz
Wyatt Taylor
Hansell Watt
Michael Wilhoit
John Wilson
Thomas F. Woods
William E. Woodward, Jr.
Harvey T. Cotten, Jr.
  Pensacola
Hampton Dunn
  Tampa
E. Robert Langley
  South Jacksonville

---

*Members of book publishing committees.

Bibliography-Books

Abernethy, Thomas Perkins. *The Burr Conspiracy*. New York: Oxford University Press, 1954.

Beebe, Elswyth Thane. *Mount Vernon is Ours: The Story of its Preservation*. New York: Duell, Sloan and Pearce, 1966.

Benton, Thomas Hart. *Thirty Years View: or a History of the Working of the American Government for Thirty Years from 1820 to 1850*. 2 vols. New York: D. Appleton and Co., 1854.

Boyd, Julian P. and Hemphill, W. Edwin. *The Murder of George Wythe: Two Essays*. Williamsburg, Virginia: Institute of Early American History and Culture, 1955.

Branch, William S. *The Eppes-Shine Families of Orange County, Florida*. Orlando: Florida Southland Printing, 1949.

Brodie, Fawn M. *Thomas Jefferson: An Intimate History*. New York: W. W. Norton, 1974.

Carter, Clarence E., ed. *The Territorial Papers*. 27 vols. Washington, D.C.: United States Government Printing Office, 1956-1960.

Cash, W. T, *Florida Becomes A State*. Tallahassee: Florida Centennial Commission, 1945.

Chidsey, Donald Barr. *The Great Conspiracy: Arron Burr and His Strange Doings in the West*. New York: Crown Publishers, 1967.

Clark, Eva Turner. *Francis Eppes: His Ancestors and Descendants*. New York: Richard R. Smith, 1942.

Cushman, Joseph D. *A Goodly Heritage*: The Episcopal Church in Florida 1821-1892. Gainesville: University of Florida Press, 1965.

Davis, Henry P. *The Modern Dog Encyclopedia*. Harrisburg, Pennsylvania: The Stackpole Co., 1953.

du Bellet, Louise Pecquet. *Some Prominent Virginia Families* 4 vols. Lynchburg, Virginia: J. P. Bell. 1907.

Eaton, Margaret. *The Autobiography of Peggy Eaton*. New York: Charles Scribner's Sons, 1932.

Ellet, Mrs. E. Fries. *Queens of American Society*. Philadelphia: Porter and Coates, 1867.

Forest, Mary. *Women of the South Distinguished in Literature*. New York: Derby and Jackson, 1861.

Freeman, Harley L. *Florida Obsolete Notes and Scrip*. Glen Ridge, New Jersey: Society of Paper Money Collectors, 1967.

Fuller, Hubert Bruce. *The Purchase of Florida*. Cleveland: Burrows Bros., Co., 1906.

Gaines, William H. *Thomas Mann Randolph: Jefferson's Son-in-Law*. Kingsport, Tenn.: Louisiana State University Press, 1966.

Gottschalk, Louis. *Lafayette and the Close of the American Revolution*. Chicago: University of Chicago Press, 1942.

Groene, Bertram H. *Ante-Bellum Tallahassee*. Tallahassee: Florida Heritage Foundation, 1971.

Hanna, A. J. *A Prince in their Midst: The Adventurous Life of Achille Murat on the American Frontier*. Norman: University of Oklahoma Press, 1946.

Kennedy, John P. *Memoirs of the Life of William Wirt: Attorney General of the United States*. 2 vols. Philadelphia: Lea and Blanchard, 1850.

Knauss, James Owen. *Territorial Florida Journalism*. DeLand, Florida: Florida State Historical Society, 1926.

Long, Ellen Call. *Florida Breezes: or Florida New and Old*. Gainesville: University of Florida Press, 1962.

Mahon, John K. *History of the Second Seminole War 1835-1842*. Gainesville: University of Florida Press, 1967.

The Memorial of Life and Services of Washington Bartlett, Late Governor of the State of California. San Francisco: Society of California Pioneers, 1888.

Paisley, Clifton. *From Cotton to Quail: An Agricultural Chronicle of Leon County, Florida 1860-1967*. Gainesville: University of Florida Press, 1968.

Phillips, Leon. *That Eaton Woman: In Defense of Peggy O'Neale Eaton*. New York: Crown Publishers, 1974.

Randolph, Sarah N. *The Domestic Life of Thomas Jefferson*. Monticello-Charlottesville: Thomas Jefferson Memorial Foundation, 1947.

Schachner, Nathan. *Thomas Jefferson: A Biography* 2 vols. New York: Appleton Century-Crofts, Inc., 1951.

Stanley, J. Randall. *The History of Gadsden County*. Quincy, Florida: Gadsden County Times, 1948.

Sutton, Leora M. *The Walton House*. Pensacola, Florida: Pensacola Historic Preservation Society, 1968.

Tebeau, Charlton W. *A History of Florida*. Coral Gables: University of Miami Press, 1971.

Webster, Fletcher, ed. *The Private Correspondence of Daniel Webster* 2 vols. Boston: Little, Brown and Co., 1857.

Willis, Adelaide Rutherford. *The Willis Family of Virginia and Some of Their Descendants*. Mobile, Alabama: Paper Work, 1967.

Woodford, Frank B. *Mr. Jefferson's Disciple: A Life of Justice Woodward*. East Lansing Michigan: The Michigan State College Press, 1953.

Woodward, William E. *Lafayette*. New York: Farrar and Rinehart, Inc., 1938.

Wright, J. Leitch, Jr. *Florida in the American Revolution*. Gainesville: University Presses of Florida, 1975.

Bibliography–
Other Sources

Abbey, Kathryn T. "The Story of the Lafayette Lands in Florida." *The Florida Historical Society Quarterly* 10 (January 1932): 115-133.

Boyd, Mark F. "Events at Prospect Bluff on the Apalachicola River, 1808-1818." The Florida Historical Quarterly 16 (October 1937): 55-96.

Brown, Elizabeth Caspar. "Judge Augustus Brevoort Woodward: Man of Property." *Michigan History* 40 (1956): 190-202.

Cuthbert, Norma B. "Poplar Forest: Jefferson's Legacy to his Grandson." *Huntington Library Quarterly* 6 (1942): 333-338.

Davis, Mary Lamar. "Tallahassee Through Territorial Days." *Apalachee* (1944): 47-61.

Dodd, Dorothy. "Horse Racing in Middle Florida." *Apalachee* (1948-1950): 20-29.

Dodd, Dorothy. "Old Tallahassee." *Apalachee* (1957-1962): 63-71.

Detroit Free Press, 28 February 1909.

Eppes, Mrs. Nicholas Ware. "Francis Eppes (1801-1881), Pioneer of Florida." *The Florida Historical Society Quarterly* 5 (October 1926): 94-102.

Florida Mirror, 29 March 1879. Fernandina, Florida.

Long, Ellen Call. "Princess Achille Murat: A Biographical Sketch." *The Florida Historical Society Quarterly* 2 (July 1909): 27-38.

Parker, Rosalind. "The Proctors—Antonio, George, and John." *Apalachee* (1946): 19-29.

Photographs and Statistics of Grand Marshals of Most Worshipful Grand Lodge F. and A.M. Issue No. 2 (1830-1973).

"The Princess Murat: Nee Catherine Dangerfield Willis." *The Household*. undated copy, Florida State Library.

Tallahassee Democrat, 7 July 1970.

Tallahassee, Florida. Manuscript copy in possession of Mrs. LeRoy Collins. Richard Keith Call. "Journal of Richard Keith Call."

Tallahassee, Florida. unpublished manuscript. Governor Thomas A.
    Brown. "Memoirs," (1863).
"Whitfield's Notes." *Florida Statutes* (1941).
Winchester, Massachusetts. unpublished manuscript. John Chipman.
    "Florida Randolphs and Related Families."

Index of Names